中英文對照 附年表　Bilingual Chinese-English Format・Timeline

台灣史入門秘笈＋最實用的台灣史英文教材

An invaluable guide to Taiwan history + A practical English-teaching aid

Ten Short Talks on Taiwan History

台灣史10講

認識台灣歷史精華讀本 上

An ideal primer on Taiwan history I

總策劃➡吳密察　台灣大學歷史系副教授
英文版策劃➡文魯彬（Robin J. Winkler）台灣蠻野心足生態協會理事長
撰文➡吳密察、陳雅文
英文審訂➡翁佳音、賴慈芸、耿柏瑞（Brian A. Kennedy）
英文翻譯➡耿柏瑞（Brian A. Kennedy）、范傑克（Jacques Van Wersch）
白啓賢（Matthew Clarke）、賴凱文（Kevin Lax）、何仁傑（Peter Hillman）
文魯彬（Robin J. Winkler）、蘇瑛珣（June Su）

目錄

Table of Contents

總策劃的話
吳密察（本書總策劃，台灣大學歷史系副教授）

　　「台灣史」納入正式基礎教育的學習內容已有多年，這無非是希望能夠教育下一代「台灣人應知台灣事」。然而，認識台灣、了解家鄉不僅是「下一代」的事，身為父母、老師、社會中堅的「這一代」或「上一代」的你和我，也應該利用機會去接觸並常常重新溫習。

　　一部深入淺出、均衡適中的歷史書，必須建立在堅實豐富的研究基礎之上，脫離政治因素的過度干涉，並跳開各種成見與思想偏執。新自然主義公司邀請我，分別策劃一套給小朋友看的漫畫版台灣史，和給大朋友看的兩本台灣簡史和台灣史小百科文字書，從遠古、荷西、鄭氏時代、清代、日本時代以及戰後六個時期，重新勾繪台灣史脈絡與全貌，相信它們提供了讓大家增進台灣歷史知識的管道。

　　我在長年教書及與外國友人交流的過程中發現，應該要有英文版的台灣史，以滿足海外僑民的需求。頻繁接觸外國友人的涉外單位及企業主，以及苦惱於不知如何精準地以英文表達台灣歷史的文史研究者，也可以利用這些書來介紹台灣。英文版在文魯彬先生（Robin J. Winkler）的召集之下，邀請中外籍專家翻譯、審校，英文可說是道地又嚴謹，讓這些書甚至還可以當作學習英語的讀本。

Message from the Editor-in-Chief
By Dr. Wu Mi-cha, Editor-in-Chief

Taiwan history was officially incorporated into the basic educational curriculum here many years ago in the hope of imparting to the next generation "what all Taiwanese should know about Taiwan." Knowledge of Taiwan's past, however, is not just a matter for the next generation. Indeed, parents, teachers, and those of us in this and the previous generation who form the core of Taiwan's society should also take every opportunity to brush up on its history.

An easy-to-read yet balanced account of history must be based on solid research and be free from political influence, preconceived notions and prejudices. Third Nature Publishing approached me with the idea of producing, in comic format for children and text format for older readers, a comprehensive overview of Taiwan history focusing on six key eras: ancient Taiwan, the European era, the Jheng rule, the Cing Dynasty, Japanese colonialism and the post-WWII era. I believe that the results of this collaboration: "A History of Taiwan in Comics," "Ten Short Talks on Taiwan History" and "Mini-Encyclopedia of Taiwan History" open up a new avenue for promoting greater understanding of Taiwan history.

Over the course of many years of teaching and exchanging views with friends abroad on the subject of Taiwan history, the need for a history of Taiwan in English has become apparent. Taiwanese businesspeople, government officials and academics abroad faced with the daunting task of communicating Taiwan history in English will find "A History

想要短時間速讀台灣史精華，想要和朋友天南地北暢談台灣史，想要和親子一起重溫昔日台灣的古早事，以及想要學英文或是想要向外國友人介紹台灣，這些書肯定是最佳的台灣史讀物。誠摯邀請大家一起來讀台灣史、了解台灣事。

of Taiwan in Comics," "Ten Short Talks on Taiwan History" and"Mini-Encyclopedia of Taiwan History" very helpful in that regard. These works, the products of the combined efforts of many local and foreign expert translators and editors under the guidance of Robin Winkler, have been translated in English to exacting standards and are therefore also excellent resources for studying English.

Whether you would like to quickly learn the essentials of Taiwan history, discuss Taiwan history with friends from afar, brush up on aspects of Taiwan's ancient history with your parents or children, study English or introduce Taiwan history to foreign friends, "A History of Taiwan in Comics," "Ten Short Talks on Taiwan History" and "Mini-Encyclopedia of Taiwan History" are your best choice. I cordially invite everyone to read these books for a greater understanding of Taiwan and its history.

編輯室報告

　　大家期待一部以淺顯易懂的筆調、立論中肯的觀點書寫的中英對照台灣史出版了。《台灣史10講》邀請台大歷史系吳密察副教授親自撰寫10則簡史，並附上台灣歷史年表；《台灣歷史小百科》則收錄65個史實與趣聞兼具的先民故事，以多面向解讀台灣。這兩本台灣史文字書，可說是寫給大朋友輕鬆認識台灣歷史的最佳入門秘笈。

　　在此，將《台灣史10講》和《台灣歷史小百科》的編輯體例說明如下：

　　一、 為力求中性敘述、符合當代思潮，本書將目前台灣的居民（Taiwanese），大別為「華人（Chinese）」和「原住民（Indigenous Peoples）」。

　　1.「華人」包括二十世紀之前移入的福佬系（或閩南系）、客家系，甚至二十世紀中期之後移入的「外省人」；一般常被稱為「漢人（Han Chinese）」，本書則均改稱為「華人」。

　　2. 一九九四年政府回應「原住民」的「正名」要求，不再稱為「山胞」，本書均改稱為「原住民」；這是個泛稱，其中因為語言、文化、社會組織等等的個別差異，可以歸類成好幾族。

　　3.「台灣人」原應泛指生活於這土地上的住民；但本書部分內容所指的「台灣人」或「台灣話」，則為因應當時代所描繪的情境，大多只狹義的指稱族群最多、

Editor's Notes

The publication of easy to read yet balanced bilingual accounts of Taiwan history such as "Ten Short Talks on Taiwan History" and "Mini-Encyclopedia of Taiwan History" has been long awaited. "Ten Short Talks on Taiwan History," written by Wu Mi-cha, associate professor with National Taiwan University's Department of History, also includes a convenient "Timelines" section. "Mini-Encyclopedia of Taiwan History" comprises 65 historical narratives loaded with facts and anecdotes providing a multi-dimensional approach to learning about Taiwan's past. These two easy to read books are wonderful introductions to the history of Taiwan.

Notes on style for "Ten Short Talks on Taiwan History" and "Mini-Encyclopedia of Taiwan History":

1. For the sake of an unbiased presentation in line with contemporary thinking, the current residents of Taiwan, or the "Taiwanese," are classified as members of two broad categories, "Chinese" and "Indigenous Peoples."

(1) "Chinese" include descendents of Fujianese (Hoklo) and Cantonese (Hakka) who immigrated to Taiwan prior to the 20th century, as well as the "waishengren," (literally "outer province people") or "mainlanders," who arrived in the mid-20th century. They are also often generally referred to as "Han Chinese," but this series refers to this group simply as "Chinese."

(2) In 1994, in response to demands from the indigenous community, the government scrapped the use of the term "mountain compatriots" to describe Taiwan's indigenous

分布最廣的福佬人（閩南人），以及該族群所慣用的語言「福佬話」（閩南話）。

　　二、　書中英文譯音均採行「通用拼音」；例外情況為台灣各縣市名、當代人名等等，則參考內政部公布的地名譯寫原則、政府年鑑、國際慣例、學術常用字等等拼注方式。

　　這兩本書的中文內容，亦同時收錄在本社出版的彩色漫畫、對白中英對照的《認識台灣歷史》套書裡（共10本），內容精采、有趣又好讀，相信是帶領小朋友穿越時空，遨遊台灣的最佳歷史漫畫書。

peoples, adopting instead the term "yuanjhumin" (literally "original residents"). This series uses that term, "yuanjhumin" in its Chinese-language text and "indigenous peoples" in the English-language text as a broad term to describe the numerous indigenous groups, which are themselves distinct based upon language, culture, social structure and other differences.

(3) Generally speaking, the term "Taiwanese" refers to all people who call Taiwan home. But to reflect the historical situations depicted in this book, "Taiwanese" is usually used in a narrower sense that refers to the largest and most widely spread group, the Fujianese, and the people who speak their Fujian dialect.

2. This series uses the Tongyong Pinyin romanization system for Chinese character spellings. Exceptions to this rule are names of Taiwan's cities and counties and some proper names for contemporary people, which are taken from the official list issued by the Ministry of the Interior, government yearbooks, customary international usage or commonly accepted academic spellings.

The Chinese text in "Ten Short Talks on Taiwan History" and "Mini-Encyclopedia of Taiwan History" also appears in the full-color, bilingual English-Chinese "A History of Taiwan in Comics" (a ten-volume set). Interesting and easy to read, these books will transport young readers on a fascinating journey through Taiwan's rich past.

【台灣歷史開講】

Let's Talk About Taiwan

台灣歷史專家吳密察副教授精心撰寫十則簡史，迅速掌握台灣歷史全貌！

These short narratives on Taiwan history, written by Taiwan historian Wu Mi-cha, help you gain a guick grasp of Taiwan history.

台灣歷史，豐富又精采

　　在台灣，一般人腦海中的地圖，大概有兩種，那就是將中心放在西亞蔥嶺一帶（歐亞大陸中心）的世界地圖，另一種則是把中心放在甘肅的中國地圖。在這兩種地圖中，台灣都會是在歐亞大陸的東南邊緣地區，這兩種地圖都是以陸地為主的地圖。但是這種以陸地為主的地圖，卻不足以充分說明早期的台灣歷史。

以海洋為中心的地圖

　　為了了解早期的台灣歷史，應該有一種將中心移到海洋的地圖，那就是把焦點放在東中國海與南中國海交接點上的台灣之地圖。從這種地圖便可以清楚的看到，在台灣的周邊展開的，不但有歐亞大陸的東緣陸地，也有歐亞大陸東緣的海洋與群島，更有廣闊的大洋海域。

　　十六世紀中葉以前，台灣並未被中國有意識地納入其視野當中，生息於台灣這個島上的居民，也與隔著台灣海峽的對岸福建不同，反而是與菲律賓、印尼等地一樣，即被十九世紀以來的民族學者稱為南島語族（Austronesian）的另一種民族。

　　南島語族的分布範圍很廣。東到南美智利西邊的復活島，西到非洲東邊的馬達

The Rich and Colorful History of Taiwan

In the minds of most Taiwanese, the map of the world is centered in central Asia near the Congling Mountains (Pamir Mountains) in the middle of the Eurasian continental landmass, and the map of China centered on Gansu in the middle of China. On both maps, Taiwan appears on the far southeastern periphery of the Eurasian landmass. Both maps are continentally oriented maps. These maps, however, do not adequately reflect Taiwan's early history.

An Oceania-Oriented Map

To understand the early history of Taiwan, the focus of the map must shift toward Taiwan's location at the confluence of the East China Sea and the South China Sea. On this map, it is immediately clear that on Taiwan's periphery lies not only the inland areas of the east coast of the Eurasian continental landmass, but also a vast maritime area scattered with oceanic archipelagos.

Prior to the mid-16th century, Taiwan was not generally a part of the Chinese consciousness, and Taiwan's inhabitants were unrelated to those living in neighboring Fujian Province on the opposite side of the Taiwan Strait. They were in fact related to the inhabitants of the Philippine and Indonesian archipelagos, members of what anthropologists have since the 19th century classified as the Austronesian group.

The dispersion area of the Austronesian linguistic group is vast, stretching from Easter

加斯加島，南到巴布亞‧新幾內亞，甚至紐西蘭，北到台灣。這是一個橫跨赤道南北，包括太平洋與印度洋的廣大海域。南島語族之所以能夠分布在如此廣闊的海域，一般的學者認為他們是依靠著季風、洋流等自然力之助，在海上移動所致。

台灣附近海域的西南季風和洋流，被認為是幫助台灣原住民遷移來台的自然力。因此，長期以來學者認為台灣原住民是在不同的時期，自不同的地方，經過不同的途徑，先後自南方來到台灣的不同地方居住下來的。

但是對於這種外來說，最近則有學者持反對的意見。因為雖然有些台灣的原住民（例如蘭嶼的達悟族）明顯是晚近才來自南方的菲律賓巴丹島，有些原住民（例如東部的阿美族）也有航海來自遠方的傳說，但卻也有些原住民顯得對海洋頗為陌生。因此，近年有些民族學者、語言學者及考古學者認為台灣反而是周邊地區南島語族的移出地。

島內居民文化具有多樣性

目前台灣的居民，雖然可大別為華人與原住民兩種，但原住民內部又可依語言、文化、社會組織等分成好幾族，華人當中也可分成福佬系、客家系，甚至「外省人」。其實台灣島上的居民自古就很複雜，在不同的時期，甚至相同時期的不同地方，也可能住著不同系統的人。這從考古學也可以得到證明。

Island off the coast of Chile in the east to Madagascar off the coast of Africa in the west, from Papua New Guinea and even as far as New Zealand in the south, to Taiwan in the north. This includes a vast area straddling both tropics and including huge swathes of the Pacific and Indian oceans. Scholars generally agree that early seasonal monsoons and oceanic currents played a role in scattering the group over so wide an area.

It is presumed that Taiwan's original inhabitants arrived under the power of the southwest monsoon and oceanic current that affects the area. Consequently, scholars have long believed that Taiwan's indigenous peoples arrived from the south at different times coming from different places and following different routes.

Some scholars, however, have recently contested this hypothesis. They argue that although some of Taiwan's indigenous tribes (such as the Tao tribe on Orchid Island) are clearly relatively recent arrivals from the Batan Islands in the Philippines and others (such as the Amis of the east coast) have folk traditions involving epic sea voyages from far off places, there are, however, some tribes that are obviously strangers to the sea. As a result, a number of anthropologists, linguists and archaeologists now argue that Taiwan is actually a point of origin for the Austronesian language group speakers in the surrounding region.

Taiwan's Multicultural Tapestry

The current inhabitants of Taiwan can be divided into two broad groups, namely, ethnic Chinese and indigenous peoples. The indigenous people can be further divided into a number of different groups based on language, culture and social organization, as can

【關鍵字】台灣原住民 Taiwan's indigenous people / 達悟族 the Tao tribe / 阿美族 the Amis tribe / 福佬人 Hoklos (southern Fujian) / 客家人 Hakkas / 外省人 mainlanders

17

目前，考古學者所知道的台灣舊石器時代遺址有兩個系統，分別是東部與南部的長濱文化和北部的網形文化。到了距今大約七千年前，則開始出現刀耕火種的游耕生產形態，進入新石器時代早期（大坌坑文化）。在距今大約五千年前，即台灣新石器中期文化，開始出現地區性的分化，這一方面是原來新石器時代早期文化的持續發展，一方面則是因為有新的外來文化移入。到了距今三千五百年前，則分化更為繁複。距今大約二千年至四千年之間，各地區以不同的程度進入鐵器時期。其中，比較晚近的十三行遺址還發現煉鐵的遺跡。雖然如此，台灣原住民的主要生產工具，在華人來到之前還是長期停留在木石併用階段，鐵器並不普遍。

十七世紀華人大規模來到之前，台灣原住民採游耕、游獵方式獲取生活所需，傳統作物有薯、芋、旱稻、小米、黍、麻等，狩獵以捕鹿為主。

Taiwan's modern Chinese inhabitants be divided into the majority descendents of early settlers from southern Fujian Province (Hoklos), the Hakkas and so-called "mainlanders." Actually, since ancient times, Taiwan's population has been complex, with completely different ethnic groups living here at differing times or during the same period but in different areas. This is borne out by archaeological finds.

Currently, archaeologists have unearthed the relics of two Paleolithic cultures in Taiwan, the Changbin Culture of eastern and southern Taiwan and the Wangsing Culture of northern Taiwan. About 7,000 years ago, hunter-gatherer cultures began to engage in slash and burn cultivation (the Dabenkeng Culture) during the early Neolithic era. Some time around 5,000 years ago, Taiwan's middle-Neolithic era cultures began to exhibit territorial distinctions, resulting from the continued development of the original early Neolithic cultures on the one hand and the arrival of new cultures from elsewhere. By 3,500 years ago, these distinctions were becoming increasingly complex. Between 2,000 and 4,000 years ago, each of these different cultures entered the Iron Age, attaining varying degrees of advancement. Of those, evidence of iron making has been found at the ruins of the relatively recent Shihsanhang Culture. Despite this, the indigenous tribes were largely using tools of stone and wood at the time of the arrival of the Chinese; iron implements were not widespread.

Prior to the arrival of large numbers of Chinese in the 17th century, Taiwan's indigenous people subsisted on slash and burn agriculture, hunting and gathering. Their traditional produce included yams, taro, dryland rice, millet, proso and hemp, while they hunted mostly deer.

【關鍵字】長濱文化 the Changbin Culture / 網形文化 the Wangsing Culture / 刀耕火種 slash and burn cultivation / 十三行文化 the Shihsanhang Culture

西洋人鍾情的貿易據點

十六世紀，東亞海域有了重大的變化。西洋的航海殖民勢力終於來到東亞地區，葡萄牙、西班牙是其先頭隊伍。尤其在十六世紀中葉以後，西班牙人占據呂宋島馬尼拉，便招致了中國東南沿海地區的人，紛紛下海貿易，成了中國史上的倭寇興盛時期（此時期的「倭寇」，絕大部分是中國人）。

台灣開始受到重視

東亞海域既然成為世界性的商業活絡地區，位於東中國海和南中國海交界的台灣，便立刻受到在此附近海域活動的冒險商人勢力的重視，成了「倭寇」貿易的落腳處。十七世紀初，荷蘭成為加入東亞貿易的新興西洋航海殖民勢力。荷蘭聯合東印度公司為了在距中國不遠的地方，尋找一個從事中國商品轉口貿易的據點，同時攔截福建前往馬尼拉貿易的華商之商業機會，在一六二四年進占福爾摩沙島的大員（今台南安平）。

荷蘭人進占台灣的最初目的，是要利用台灣做為中國貿易的據點，在此買進中國的生絲、瓷器，然後轉賣日本、歐洲各地。但是，後來也逐漸在台灣發展農墾事

A Favorite European Trade Stronghold

The maritime areas of East Asia witnessed enormous changes in the 16th century. Western maritime powers had finally arrived in East Asia, with Portugal and Spain in the vanguard. In the mid-16th century, Spain stepped up its colonial effort, occupying Manila and attracting a lot of Chinese traders from the southeast coastal region. Acts of piracy by the so-called Wako (literally "Japanese pirates") in the area peaked around this time (although the majority of the "Japanese pirates" of that era were actually Chinese).

Taiwan Gets Noticed

As East Asia emerged as a hotspot of global trade, Taiwan, located along trading routes between the East China Sea and the South China Sea, quickly attracted the attention of adventurous merchant-traders. Pirates commonly used Taiwan as a refuge for rest and re-supply. In the early 17th century, The Dutch emerged as a new maritime power in East Asia. The Dutch East India Company (*Verenigde Oostindische Compagnie*, or Dutch VOC) sought a location close to the Chinese mainland to serve as a transshipment point for Chinese goods and from which to intercept Fujianese commercial traffic bound for Manila in the Philippines. In 1624, they landed at Tayoung (present-day Anping, Tainan) on the island of Formosa.

At first the Dutch wanted to use Taiwan as a foothold from which to conduct trade with China. From there, they purchased raw silk and porcelain from China to sell it in Japan and Europe. Gradually, they set up agricultural operations on Formosa. For this

【關鍵字】倭寇 Wako ("Japanese pirates") / 荷蘭聯合東印度公司 the Dutch East India Company (*Verenigde Oostindische Compagnie*, or Dutch VOC) / 福爾摩沙 Formosa / 大員 Tayoung

業。於是，聯合東印度公司自福建引入契約華工，耕種以生產甘蔗、稻米為主的公司農園。這是中國人大量移入台灣的開始。

荷蘭人發展農業及傳教

荷蘭人除了在台灣進行轉口貿易，發展農業生產，將台灣生產的蔗糖賣往日本、波斯，稻米賣往缺糧的中國之外，台灣的鹿產也是重要的出口品（鹿肉輸往中國，鹿皮輸往日本）。除此之外，聯合東印度公司也對前來台灣捕鹿、從事「番產交易」、捕魚的中國人課徵許可稅；對來自中國的農業工人，課徵人頭稅。聯合東印度公司在台灣的收益，頗為可觀。

聯合東印度公司對台灣的原住民（此處所謂的原住民，大部分居住於西部平原地帶）傳教。為了傳教的需要，荷蘭的傳教士學習原住民的語言，並且還將聖經翻譯成原住民語，教導原住民使用拼音字母寫自己的語言，據說在台南附近的傳教事業頗為成功。就在荷蘭占據台灣南部之後不久的一六二六年，西班牙也從馬尼拉北上，占據了台灣北部的基隆、淡水一帶。但西班牙的勢力此時已呈退潮，只能在台灣北部傳播天主教，而且不久之後（一六四四年）也被荷蘭人逐退了。

purpose, they needed to recruit contract laborers from Fujian Province in China to cultivate sugarcane and rice for the company. This marked the beginning of the mass of Chinese immigration to Taiwan.

The Development of Agriculture and the Spread of Christianity Under the Dutch Rule

The Dutch East India Company sold sugar in Japan and Persia. Rice was exported to China, which was then experiencing a rice shortage. Deerskins and other deer products were also key exports. The venison was sent to China and the hides were exported to Japan. Other income was derived from various forms of taxation: hunting, trading, and fishing were all taxed, and a poll tax was levied on Chinese workers. The Dutch East India Company made a considerable income from its Taiwan operations.

The Dutch East India Company also brought their religion to the indigenous peoples of Taiwan (mostly plains indigenous tribes living in western Taiwan). Dutch missionaries learned to speak indigenous languages and translated the Bible into the local languages. They also taught the indigenous peoples to write their language using a romanization system they devised. Their missionary efforts in the Tainan area reportedly enjoyed considerable success. Not long after the arrival of the Dutch in southern Taiwan, the Spanish arrived from Manila, establishing strongholds at Keelung and Danshuei in northern Taiwan in 1626. Spanish supremacy was, however, waning. The spread of Catholicism was confined to northern Taiwan and not long afterward (1644), the Spanish were expelled by the Dutch.

【關鍵字】人頭稅 poll tax

鄭氏集團經營台灣

　　就在荷蘭聯合東印度公司出現在東亞地區的同時，閩南地方也誕生了一位梟雄性的人物，那便是鄭芝龍。鄭芝龍生於十七世紀前夕，年輕時曾赴澳門，也充當荷蘭人的翻譯並與荷蘭人有生意往來，後來則移居日本，以平戶、長崎為據點發展勢力。

　　一六二六年，他繼承了東亞海域的龐大華人勢力。接著，又接受明朝官府的招撫，獲得了在明朝官府中的合法性。於是，鄭芝龍一方面以明朝官員的身分，剷除福建一帶的其他海上勢力；一方面又得以登陸，在中國內陸收購商品出口。因此，鄭芝龍立刻成為稱霸中國東南一帶的絕大勢力。滿清入關後，中國東南的南明政權便多賴他的支持才得以苟延一時。

　　但是，當清軍逐漸進逼南下之後，鄭芝龍卻在一六四六年投降了清朝。鄭氏集團的勢力由鄭成功接掌。鄭成功所要面對的難題，除了要整合父親留下來的勢力之外，更要應對清朝政府軟硬兼施的壓力與進逼，甚至由於與清軍長期對峙而造成的軍心離散、兵員叛逃，還有清方的堅壁清野斷絕沿海接濟。為了挽回局勢，一六五

Taiwan under the Jheng

About the time the Dutch East India Company first appeared in Southeast Asia, southern Fujian gave birth to an ambitious adventurer Jheng Jhihlong, also known as "Nicolas Iquan Cheng" in European documents. Jheng Jhilong was born at the close of the 16th century, and in his youth, went to Macau. As a young man, he interpreted for and conducted business with the Dutch. He later traveled to Japan, where his power continued to develop around his bases in Hirado and Nagasaki.

In 1626, he assumed leadership of the maritime power among an impressive network of East Asian Chinese traders, illegal at that time. Later, the patronage of the Ming Government legitimized his status. Consequently, Jheng Jhihlong on one hand utilized his position as an official to eliminate rival maritime powers around the Fujian region, and on the other controlled the export of goods from inland China. Thus Jheng Jhihlong quickly became a formidable power in southeast China. After the invasion of the Manchu, the Southern Ming Court became increasingly dependent upon his support to prolong their existence.

With Cing forces gradually pressing southward, Jheng Jhihlong surrendered and submitted to the new rulers in 1646. His son, Jheng Chenggong (also known as Koxinga), became the new leader of the Jheng bloc. In addition to consolidating the power left by his father, Jheng Chenggong had to deal with mounting pressure from Cing forces. The

【關鍵字】鄭芝龍 Jheng Jhihlong (Nicolas Iquan Cheng) / 鄭氏集團 the Jheng bloc / 鄭成功（國姓爺）Jheng Chenggong (Koxinga) / 清朝 the Cing dynasty (also know as Ching or Qing)

25

九年鄭成功發動大軍北伐，攻入長江流域，雖曾暫時獲勝，但卻因指揮錯誤而敗回閩南之金門、廈門。翌年，退守金廈之鄭成功，受到南下清軍之重創，而且糧餉匱乏，於是在一六六一年率軍渡海來台找尋休養生息的機會。

鄭成功選擇台灣休養生息

　　一六六一年三月，鄭成功率軍攻台，經過數個月與荷蘭人的對峙，該年十二月十三日（陽曆一六六二年二月一日）迫使荷蘭投降退出台灣，結束三十八年的統治。但是，鄭成功在不久之後的一六六二年五月八日病逝。

　　鄭成功病逝之後，其子鄭經繼位，雖仍希望保有海峽對岸之閩南地方，但並未能實現。一六七三年，吳三桂等人反抗清朝政府削藩，在中國東南地方發動「三藩之亂」，鄭經趁機反攻大陸，一時之間頗有斬獲，但也在一六八〇年敗退台灣。翌年，鄭經去世，鄭氏集團內訌。相對地，清朝方面則任命主張積極討伐台灣的施琅為福建水師提督，伺機對台用兵。一六八三年六月，施琅率軍攻台，澎湖戰役鄭軍大敗；八月，施琅率軍登陸台灣、鄭克塽投降。

建立台灣首次的華人政權

　　鄭氏自鄭芝龍歷經鄭成功到鄭經以迄鄭克塽的四代三世的八十年間，代表一個活力充沛的閩南海商集團的興起與崩潰。這個興衰歷程的背景，則又有西洋東來的

morale of his troops was low and many deserted as a result of the long-term standoff. Cing forces also sought to cut him off from aid provided by the coastal regions. To counter Cing actions, Jheng Chenggong mounted a northern campaign in 1659, invading the Lower Yangtze River region. After initial successes, his tactical mistakes forced him to retreat to Kinmen and Siamen in southern Fujian. The following year, Cing forces launched new attacks on Kinmen and Siamen. In addition, the Jheng camp suffered from a shortage of provisions. Consequently, in 1661, Jheng sailed for Taiwan, hoping for a chance to rest and regroup.

Koxinga Decides to Rest and Regroup in Taiwan

In the third lunar month of 1661, Jheng Chenggong's troops attacked Taiwan, then occupied by the Dutch. After several months of stiff resistance, the Dutch capitulated on 1 February 1662 and left Taiwan, ending 38 years of rule. But Jheng Chenggong died of illness on the fifth lunar month of the next year (also 1662).

Jheng Jing succeeded his father, Chenggong, and attempted to again seize control the coastal area of Fujian across the Taiwan Strait, but failed to achieve his objectives. In 1673, former Ming general Wu Sanguei and others revolted against the Cing Court, initiating the "Revolt of the Three Feudatories" in southeast China. Jheng Jing seized the opportunity to land on China, and was successful for a time, but ultimately retreated to Taiwan in 1680. The following year, when Jheng Jing died, the Jheng clan underwent an internal power struggle. At this time, Jheng's rival Shih Lang was appointed admiral by the Cing Government and commissioned to attack Taiwan. In the sixth month of Kangsi Year 22 (1683), Shih Lang led the navy in an attack, resulting in a major defeat of Jheng forces at Penghu. In the eighth month, Shih Lang led his troops against Taiwan proper,

【關鍵字】鄭經 Jheng Jing / 三藩之亂 the Revolt of the Three Feudatories / 施琅 Shih Lang / 鄭克塽 Jheng Keshuang / 海商集團 maritime trading bloc

殖民勢力和明清兩朝的鼎革。鄭氏集團也從海商而成為明朝方面的大員,又為支撐南明家業的割據勢力,最後來到台灣創立新政府。

　　鄭成功之入台,雖是其在中國沿海局勢失利下的消極轉進行為,但對台灣歷史卻有積極的意義。在此之前的台灣,是南島語族系原住民的生息天地,數十年前由荷蘭等西方殖民勢力占領,由於發展熱帶栽培業而引入福建的華工,其情形與爪哇等東南亞地方實無兩樣。但鄭成功集團來到台灣,卻使台灣有了一個華人的政權,華人也從此源源不斷地移來台灣,台灣變成了華人在數量上超過原住民的新社會。

and Jheng Keshuang, Jheng Jing's son, surrendered.

First Chinese Government in Taiwan

The eighty-year period of the Jheng clan, spanning four generations beginning with Jheng Jhihlong, passing through Jheng Chenggong to Jheng Jing and ending with Jheng Keshuang, represents the rise and collapse of a vibrant maritime trading bloc from southern Fujian. This saga was played out against a backdrop of Western colonizers, who had recently arrived in the east, as well as two Chinese dynasties. The Jheng clan began as a maritime trading bloc, transformed into powerful officials of the Ming Court in exile, and eventually came to Taiwan as rulers.

Jheng Chenggong was initially forced to retreat to Taiwan, but his arrival altered the history of Taiwan in significant ways. Prior to his arrival, Taiwan was home to indigenous tribes who spoke Austronesian languages. Although the Dutch and other colonizers from Europe had occupied the island for decades and imported Chinese labors from Fujian for tropical cultivation, the situation in Taiwan was very much like those in Java and other Southeast Asian areas. With the arrival of the Jheng military-trading bloc, however, a Chinese-style government was brought to Taiwan for the first time. The Chinese continued to immigrate to Taiwan, and Taiwan eventually became a society where the Chinese outnumbered the indigenous population.

充滿無限生機的新天地

　　清帝國以大軍屈服了鄭氏在台灣的勢力之後，並不積極要把台灣納入版圖。對清朝政府來說，重要的是消滅了一個反抗勢力，但是對於要將一海之隔，而且曾為紅毛、倭寇、海盜所窩占的台灣納入統治，卻相當消極。所以多數朝廷官員主張遷民墟地，將已來到台灣的華人遣回大陸。

　　但是施琅卻不同意這種看法。施琅出身閩南，早年也是出洋下海通販之徒，他深知閩南人必定千方百計向外謀求發展，而台灣具有各種優越條件，必定會是大家趨之若鶩的目標。而且如果不將台灣納入版圖，西洋各國也將會據之以招致華人前來貿易，那麼台灣也將成為中國東南沿海的隱憂；所以積極主張應將台灣收入版圖。最後清朝政府終於採納施琅的看法，將台灣納入版圖，設台灣府，置於福建省之下。

台灣納入大清版圖

　　清帝國雖然將台灣納入版圖，但政府最關心的是勿使台灣成為「逋逃之淵籔」，反政府的巢穴，所以在制度上設了很多防範的措施。首先，在台灣「編查流寓」，進行戶口登錄，而且將無家室、田產者遣返大陸；自大陸來台也必須申請渡航許

The Land of Boundless Potential

After defeating the Jheng clan on Taiwan, the Cing Government initially showed no intention of bringing Taiwan into it's empire. So far as the Cing Government was concerned, it's main mission on Taiwan had been simply to overcome a rebellious power. It was in no hurry to extend it's rule over a land that lay across the sea and was a hotbed of "red-hair barbarian," Japanese and Chinese pirates. Therefore, the majority of imperial court officials advocated having all the Chinese residents of Taiwan sent back to the mainland and the island abandoned.

However, Admiral Shih Lang protested this policy. He was a native of southern Fujian and in his younger years had sailed to seas in search of trading adventure. He deeply believed that the Hoklos (southern Fujianese), by their very nature, would use any means available to spread out and develop new areas. Taiwan was an area perfectly suited for development; it was certain to be a highly sought after prize. More importantly, he was convinced that if Taiwan were not brought into the Cing Empire, Western countries would move in and induce Chinese to come to the island to trade. When this happened, Taiwan would again be a potential trouble spot for the Cing Government. For these reasons, Shih aggressively advocated making Taiwan a part of the Cing Empire. In the end, the Imperial Court saw the strength of Shih's view. Taiwan Prefecture was created and placed under the jurisdiction of Fujian Province.

Joining the Empire

Even after bringing Taiwan into the empire, the Cing Government's main concern was

【關鍵字】紅毛 red-hair barbarian (mostly refered to the Dutch) / 台灣府 Taiwan Prefecture

可，透過這種出入境管理篩檢危險份子；即使被允許來台灣，也不許攜帶家眷，這種規定具有使家眷留在大陸當人質的意味。

清朝政府不但管制大陸人來台，也不歡迎來到台灣的移民積極擴大開墾空間，那是因為惟恐移民進入台灣山區無法掌控，而且也怕移民侵入山區將造成原住民的反撲。所以清朝政府在台灣西部平原地帶的東緣劃了一道境界線，禁止移民越出開墾。因此雖說清帝國將台灣納入版圖，但其統治實際上仍僅限於西部。

清朝政府為防範台灣人反抗，自中國大陸派遣軍隊來台駐紮。但又惟恐這些在台軍隊鞭長莫及，不聽中央號令，因此在軍制上頗費周章。在台軍隊以自大陸之不同營伍抽調部分人員組成，來到台灣後也分散駐防，並且三年一換，為的是使軍隊不能坐大和在地生根。清朝政府也不准在台募兵，怕台灣人當兵會使將帥無法約束。

前仆後繼渡台

雖然清朝政府的態度消極，但閩南、粵東的居民，卻一方面迫於內地生計困難，一方面垂涎台灣豐厚的生產條件，而蜂擁來台。台灣的土壤、氣候、水文都極適合當時最主要的農業生產。例如，清朝地方官便盛讚台灣：「土地肥沃、不糞

to prevent Taiwan from becoming a hideout for wanted criminals and a breeding ground for anti-Cing forces. Hence the Cing Government created policies aimed at identifying, controlling, and removing any potentially rebellious parties on Taiwan. For example, the government ordered all emigrants to submit their family registers; men without families or land were forced to return to the mainland. In order to sift out people who might be dangerous, people who wanted to sail to Taiwan were required to apply for an entry permit The lucky few who obtained permits were not allowed to bring their families, and their wives and children remained on the mainland as "hostages."

The Cing Government not only kept a firm grip on the number of people entering Taiwan, but also discouraged the settlers from expanding cultivation further. The government believed that if the spread of land cultivation were left unchecked, the Chinese settlers would spread out into the mountains where they would be difficult to control. The Cing also feared that the indigenous people would retaliate if the Chinese penetrated too deeply into their lands. Therefore, the government drew a line on the east edge of the western plains and prohibited Chinese from crossing it. As a result of this policy, even though Taiwan was officially part of the Cing Empire, the Cing only controlled the western part of the island.

To discourage and suppress rebellious activities, the Cing Government maintained a garrison on Taiwan. Fearing that the loyalty of the soldiers might waver once separated from the central authority, the government took measures to ensure that troops would not become too attached to Taiwan. Each soldier's term of duty was limited to three years, and the garrison comprised troops from different camps on the mainland. Any loyalties that developed during the journey were destroyed after reaching Taiwan, when the troops were broken up and reorganized. The Cing Government also enacted a law against recruiting soldiers from among the residents of Taiwan, fearing that military units comprising local troops would be difficult to control.

【關鍵字】渡航許可 entry permit

種，糞則穗重而仆。種植後聽其自生，惟享坐穫，每每數倍內地。」即使不是來台耕種，也有甚多工作機會：「漳泉內地無籍之民，無可耕之田，無可傭之工，無可覓之食，一到台地，上可致富，下可溫飽。一切農工商賈以至百藝之末，計工授值，比之內地，率皆倍蓰。」

　　但是，積極想渡海來台追求更好生活的閩南、粵東人士，卻未必都能獲得官府批准來台，因此只好以各種非法方法，例如買通守口官員私放、假冒漁民矇混出海，甚至由「人蛇」安排偷渡。偷渡來台的過程中，或者三番兩次被不肖之徒所騙，或者喪身海底，甚至已來到台灣又被官府捕獲強制遣返，歷經辛酸。所以，雖然「台灣錢淹腳目」，但「唐山過台灣，心肝結歸丸」。

The Endless Tide of Immigrants

Even though the Cing Government was not eager to make Taiwan part of its empire, mainlanders from the coastal areas of Fujian and Guangdong ceaselessly poured across the Taiwan Strait. They came to escape the poverty of their homeland and to take advantage of Taiwan's abundant natural resources. Taiwan's soil, climate and precipitation provided optimal conditions for farming. One Cing official praised the soil of Taiwan as being "so rich it does not need compost for fertilizer. If fertilized, the stalks of rice grow top-heavy and fall over. After you've planted the rice, all you have left to do is sit back and wait for harvest time, when you can expect several times the crop you had on the mainland ..." For those who were not farmers, there were also many opportunities on Taiwan. According to the official, "Those from Jhangjhou and Cyuanjhou prefectures in Fujian, who have no land to work, no employment and nothing to eat, can become rich, or at least support themselves, once they come to Taiwan. Farmers, craftsmen, businessmen and petty workers who came to Taiwan could expect to be rewarded for their work and earn more than they could have back home."

Accounts such as this encouraged enterprising Hoklo (southern Fujianese) and Hakka (from eastern Guangdong Province) seeking better lives to cross the Taiwan Strait. Unfortunately, many were unable to obtain Taiwan entry permits from the government and were forced to use illegal means. Some disguised themselves as fishermen, some bribed the harbor officials, and some paid off professional smugglers of illegal immigrants. History records tragic stories of those who died at sea, those who were cheated time and again by immigrant smugglers, and those who managed to make it to Taiwan only to be captured and sent back to the mainland. Thus, while for some, "Taiwan's riches run ankle deep," for others their "bitterness hardened like a stone since leaving for Taiwan."

【關鍵字】人蛇 professional smugglers ("snake heads") / 偷渡客 illegal immigrants

活力充沛的移墾社會

　　台灣的豐饒富庶，吸引了閩南、粵東的居民蜂擁來台。就像一般的新拓殖地區一樣，率先前來的多是好勇鬥狠的單身男子，這些人無田產、家室，充滿活力，熱情、勇敢、豪放，成群結黨，甚至歃血為盟。官府的控制力，在這樣的邊區移墾社會中，也相對比較薄弱，因此自然會出現以膽識、腕力為尚的土豪型人物活躍的空間。當然，這些土豪型人物在發展到相當勢力之後，也會以應科舉或捐納的方式，求得具有鄉紳的身分，並與官府有所交通。這些兼具豪、紳兩種性格的地方有力人士，既可以是橫行鄉曲的惡霸，也可能在鄉里排難解紛、造福鄉里。

土豪、鄉紳維繫社會秩序

　　由於官府的掌控力量較弱，而且也未能快速、積極仲裁社會中的糾紛，來台移民也有以原鄉地緣關係，或血緣宗親關係聚居，互通聲氣的傾向。因此，細故相爭或利益衝突時，往往也會演變成較大規模的分類械鬥。清代社會中的治安維持、防衛，也要由鄉庄自己擔任。因此，以村落為單位的武裝化，或聯合數村的攻守同盟（聯庄），成為普遍的現象。

An Energetic Settlement Community

Taiwan offered rich natural resources and a comfortable life, attracting swarms of immigrants from China's southern Fujian and eastern Guangdong regions. As is typically the case with pioneers, the first immigrants to Taiwan were a brave, swashbuckling lot, who arrived without assets or families, but bursting with energy, passion and courage. They formed gangs and sealed pacts of brotherhood among themselves with blood oaths. Because the Cing Empire exerted only weak control over Taiwan, one of its remote outlying areas, an opportunity emerged for men who used boldness and brute force to become local strongmen. After consolidating their power and influence locally, these local strong-men would seek a stamp of legitimacy in the form of a title from the government, which they could gain by making donations or participating in examinations, thus establishing an association with the government. While these local strongmen, part gentleman and part gangster, were sometimes bullies and despots with the run of their territories, they could also be skilled arbitrators of disagreements and even benefactors of the local citizenry.

Maintaining Order in Society

Because of the Cing Government's limited control over Taiwan, it could not provide prompt, effective resolution of problems and disputes. Taiwanese society at this time consisted of many small villages, each settled by Chinese who shared a common ancestry or hometown. When a confrontation occurred between two such groups over a major conflict of interest or even a trivial disagreement, it often escalated into large-scale armed feuding. And because responsibility for maintaining public order in Cing society fell to the localities anyway, villages took up arms and entered into mutual defense alliances with other villages.

【關鍵字】歃血為盟 sealed pacts of brotherhood amomg themselves with blood oaths /土豪 local strongmen / 械鬥 armed feuding / 聯庄 mutual defense alliances with other villages

至於官府與社會之間的關係，一般來說是相互疏遠的。只要不是對政權的正面攻擊，官府便不積極介入社會；社會也不積極挑釁政權。清朝時代台灣幾次比較重大的抗官事件，反而多有社會本身矛盾的影子潛藏其中，這些社會矛盾如果被政治性地運用，或政權過度敏感地打壓社會，才會爆發對政權的正面攻擊。

閩南、粵東的人，前仆後繼渡海來台，台灣的田園開闢也迅速展開。尤其清初又有不少在台官吏、豪強招徠移民進行大規模的農墾。鄭氏時期，移民之農墾區大致仍在台南一帶（北至嘉義，南至高雄），但清領五十年後的十八世紀中葉，已向北推進到彰化一帶；十八世紀中葉以後，更達台中平原北緣，來自中國大陸的移民人數也大量增加。

壓迫原住民的生活空間

華人移入人口大幅增加，及墾殖田園面積快速擴大，使原本居住於西部平地地帶的原住民（平埔族）承受了深重的壓迫。雖然清朝政府限制移民只能在「無主荒地」上進行開墾，而且也不可購買平埔族的土地，但實際上並沒有能力貫徹執行法令，因此平埔族的土地被移民以買賣、欺騙等手段不斷蠶食，終至幾乎淨盡。

這些住在平原地帶的平埔族，由於居住於清帝國所劃定的「版圖」之內，移民的村落與其錯雜相間，因此很早便被清朝政府納入統治（清朝政府稱這種接受統治

Generally speaking, the government and the settlers kept their distance from each other. As long as it was not directly challenged, the government would not actively impose its will on society, and society, in turn, avoided aggressive provocation of the government. The few serious revolts against the government that did occur were mostly instigated by the elements of social rivalries. A challenge to the Cing regime would be triggered only when these elements were manipulated for political gain, or when the regime itself became unnecessarily oppressive in exerting its control.

As immigrant farmers from southern Fujian and eastern Guangdong poured into Taiwan, the island's land development progressed by leaps and bounds. Cultivation of the land shifted into high gear in the early Cing, when government officials and wealthy settlers began soliciting settlers to engage in the development of large parcels of land. During the period in which the Jheng clan ruled the island, agricultural development by Chinese immigrants took place mostly in the Tainan area, extending to Chiayi in the north and Kaohsiung in the south. But 50 years later, during the mid-18th century, the northern border stretched to the Changhua area, and later in that century, it reached all the way to the northern edge of the Taichung Plain as the immigrant population from the mainland swelled to a new high.

Squeezing the Living Space of Indigenous Peoples

The constant influx of Chinese immigrants and rapid development of land put enormous pressure on the indigenous peoples living in the western flatlands. Officially the Cing Government prohibited the buying and selling of indigenous lands by Chinese people, restricting their claims to unowned land, but in reality it lacked the power to enforce these decrees. Uninhibited by the law, the land-hungry Chinese bought, traded, and tricked the plains indigenous people out of their land until virtually all the indigenous territory in the west had been picked clean.

【關鍵字】平埔族 the plains indigenous people

的原住民為「熟番」；相對地，稱居住於統治地區之外的原住民為「生番」)。清朝政府在這些「熟番」部落中設通事，做為傳達政令、管束原住民的中介人，「熟番」雖然可以不繳田賦，但要服「役」。役的負擔及來自通事的需索、欺壓，也使「熟番」處境困難。

受到清朝政府與華人移民的侵入壓迫，「熟番」很難在其原居地繼續如常存活下去，不但土地逐漸流失轉手給移民，文化上也逐漸被移民所同化。有些「熟番」被逼只好離開原居地進行遷徙。十八世紀末，台中平原一帶的「熟番」遷入埔里盆地，台南一帶的「熟番」越過山脈遷入東部，新開發的宜蘭平原之「熟番」往花蓮地方遷移，這些是比較有名的例子。

十九世紀初，客家人在桃竹苗一帶的發展，是個明顯的現象。這個地區的開墾主要有兩種形態，即屯墾與隘墾。屯墾是林爽文之亂平定後（一七八八年），清朝政府將原來位於「界外」的部分地區，劃為名目上屬於「熟番」屯丁所有的屯地，讓移民可以向「熟番」佃耕這些土地。隘墾則是在靠近「生番」地域墾殖時，同時由開墾集團設武裝防禦性的「隘」，以防止「生番」出草。

The western flatlands lay within the area the Cing Government designated for settlement by Chinese immigrants, and indigenous peoples living in these areas had to accept Cing Government rule. The Cing Government dubbed such indigenous peoples "cooked tribes," while those who lived outside Cing territory and denied Cing rule were called "raw tribes". The Cing assigned each cooked tribe an "interpreter" whose responsibility was to relay government orders and keep the indigenous peoples in check. Although the cooked tribesmen were exempt from taxes, they were required to perform corvee labor for the government. This placed the tribesmen at the beck and call of the often tyrannical "interpreters."

To the cooked tribesmen the arrival of the Cing Government and the Chinese settlers was an invasion of their land and lifestyle. Not only did indigenous territory gradually fall into the hands of the settlers, their culture slowly crumbled and was replaced by that of the Chinese. Some of the cooked tribesmen were forced to leave their original places of residence: at the end of the 18th century, the migration of the Taichung cooked tribemen to Puli, the Tainan cooked tribemen crossing the mountains to the eastern part of Taiwan, and the Yilan cooked tribe moving to Hualien are some well-known examples.

In the beginning of the 19th century, the Hakkas developed land widely in the Miaoli area. There were two main forms of agriculture being undertaken in this area: military settlement farming and "guard-post farming." After the revolt of Lin Shuangwun was put down in 1788, the Cing Government legalized the rental of certain cooked tribe lands that had been decreed off-limits to Chinese settlers. The land stayed in the tribesmen's hands, but the Chinese were allowed to rent it. The guard-post farming system was used to reclaim lands near the raw tribes. Land development groups stationed guards in fortress-like defense garrisons to protect farmers against attack by raw tribesmen.

【關鍵字】熟番 cooked tribes / 生番 raw tribes / 屯墾 military settlement farming / 隘墾 guard-post farming /
林爽文之亂 Lin Shuangwen Revolt / 界外 off-limits

清帝國開始重視台灣

　　十九世紀中葉，西方的工業先進國家積極前來遠東尋求貿易機會。清帝國仍然固守祖宗成法，不准非朝貢國前來貿易，終於引發了有名的鴉片戰爭。鴉片戰爭的結果，不但使英國領有了香港殖民地，而且中國也開放五個港口與外國通商；西方國家終於打開了中國的門戶。

各國窺伺的貿易據點

　　在中國東南沿海門戶地方的台灣，當然暴露在新一波的遠東國際貿易熱潮當中。台灣海峽再度成為國際貿易船隻來往絡繹的海道。西方各國偶爾有船隻在台灣海面遭遇海難，或也希望在台灣找到停泊補給的口岸，對於台灣的開放也抱持強烈期待。一八六〇年，英法聯軍之役後的天津條約終於打開了台灣的門戶。清帝國開放了台灣南北的安平、滬尾（淡水）做為口岸，從此外國商人可以來台買賣，傳教士也再度來台傳教。

　　一八七四年，日本明治政府為了轉移國內沒落士族的不滿，以琉球人被台灣原住民殺害為理由，出兵攻打台灣恆春半島。清朝政府原本對此問題採消極推諉態度，當日本興兵後才派沈葆楨來台交涉。日本的征台軍因多罹患風土病而答應退

The Cing Empire Begins to Value Taiwan

Around the middle of the 19th century, the advanced industrialized nations of the West were aggressively seeking trade opportunities in the Far East. The imperial Cing Court stubbornly clung to tradition and refused to trade with those not from tribute states, eventually sparking the well-known Opium Wars. The Opium Wars resulted not only in the cession of Hong Kong as a British colony but also the opening of five treaty ports to foreign trade. The West had finally pried open the gate of China.

Foreign Countries Eye Trading Strongholds

At the gateway to China's southeast coast, Taiwan was of course swept up in the new international fever for trade with the Far East. The Taiwan Strait once again became a major maritime thoroughfare for international trade. The nations of the West, which occasionally lost ships in the waters around Taiwan, harbored a strong desire to open Taiwan as a port of call for resupply of their ships. The Treaty of Tianjin, imposed by the Anglo-French Alliance, finally opened Taiwan in 1860. The Cing Empire opened the Taiwan ports of Anping in the south and Huwei (Danshuei) in the north. Henceforth, foreign merchants were free to trade in Taiwan, missionaries also reappeared.

In 1874, Japan's Meiji Government, seeking to soothe discontent among its declining samurai class, attacked Taiwan's Hengchun Peninsula on the pretext that several Okinawa islanders had been killed by Taiwan indigenous people. The Cing Government initially adopted a head-in-the-sand attitude toward the issue, dispatching Shen Baojhen for nego-

---

【關鍵字】朝貢國 tribute states / 鴉片戰爭 the Opium Wars / 英法聯軍 the Anglo-French Alliance / 日本士族（武士）samurai class / 沈葆楨 Shen Baojhen

出，但此事件讓清朝政府改變清初以來認定台灣之亂事「將起於內，而非起於外」的看法，開始重視海防，而且解除大陸與台灣之間的渡航禁令，撤廢進入東部山區的封山政策，甚至還鼓勵往東部殖民。

開港之後，西洋商人前來台灣購買的商品大宗是茶、糖與樟腦。砂糖原本便是台灣平原地帶的重要產品，長久以來販運中國內地。茶則是在一八六○年代以後才發展起來，主要集中栽植於淡水河上游的山坡地。樟腦的產地則在台中以北，桃竹苗的淺山丘陵地區。茶、樟腦的新產業，使台中以北的的淺山丘陵地區，在這個時候快速拓墾開來。因此，沈葆楨在一八七○年代的開山政策，應該也是因應產業新趨勢的必然措施。

台灣升格設省

一八八四年中法戰爭也波及到台灣來，法國不但對基隆發動砲擊，而且在淡水登陸作戰，又以艦隊封鎖台灣。清朝政府派劉銘傳來台籌辦防務。戰後，劉銘傳在基隆、淡水、澎湖等港口要地建設砲台，並建議清朝政府在台灣設省。一八八五年，清朝政府決定在台灣設省，從此台灣島內自設三府，不再隸屬福建省管轄，劉銘傳為首任巡撫。

劉銘傳任台灣巡撫後，積極在台灣進行洋務建設，舉其大者有：興建從基隆至

tiations only after the Japanese had sent their army. The Japanese occupation forces, many weakened by local disease, eventually agreed to withdraw. This incident, however, prompted a change in a long-held tenet regarding Taiwan affairs, (going back to the early Cing) that the source of trouble with Taiwan came from within, rather than without. Afterwards, the Cing Government put greater emphasis on Taiwan's maritime defense, lifted the ban on travel between the island and the mainland, ended the policy barring entry into the east coast mountain areas, and even encouraged settlement there.

Following the opening of the ports, Western merchants came to Taiwan to trade mostly for tea, sugar and camphor. Raw sugar was the chief product of the flatland areas of Taiwan and had long been sold in markets in the interior of China. Tea wasn't grown until the 1860s and was cultivated on slope land along the upper reaches of the Danshuei River. Camphor was harvested in the region north of Taichung, in the foothills around the Miaoli, Hsinchu and Taoyuan areas. The new tea and camphor industries sparked the rapid cultivation and settlement of the foothills of northern Taiwan, from Taichung to Taipei. Consequently, Shen Baojhen's policy of exploiting the mountains in the 1870s can also be seen as a necessary measure to meet the changing commercial trends.

Taiwan Becomes a Province

In 1884, the Sino-French War spread to Taiwan, with the French not only shelling Keelung and landing in Huwei, but also blockading the island. The Cing Government sent Liu Mingchuan to organize Taiwan's defenses. Following the war, Liu constructed forts at Keelung, Huwei and Penghu, while recommending that the Cing Government establish Taiwan as a full province. In 1885, the Cing Government recognized Taiwan as

新竹的鐵路，興建郵傳、電報系統，經營輪船往來香港、福建與台灣之間，建設北台灣商業中心的大稻埕，整飭洋商交易規範，開設軍械局、機器局。

但劉銘傳的各項建設都必須有財政的支持始得為之。劉銘傳籌措經費的辦法，一是進行土地清丈，將隱匿未課稅的耕地清出，增加田賦收入；一是與台灣士紳合作，由士紳投資官府的新事業。但劉銘傳也將不少利權交給士紳們，例如板橋林家與霧峰林家，都有不少開山與樟腦利權。

劉銘傳時期的另一項重要施政，是積極的「開山撫番」。隨著茶、樟腦產業的發展，華人積極進入山地，造成對原住民的壓迫；而劉銘傳與台灣的豪紳，為了獲取山地的資源，發動了頻繁的「征番戰爭」。

a full province. Henceforth, Taiwan was divided into three prefectures and no longer under the jurisdiction of the Fujian authorities. Liu Mingchuan was appointed the first governor of the new province.

After taking office, Liu set to work on Taiwan's commercial and transport infrastructure. His projects included laying a railroad between Keelung and Hsinchu; establishing postal and telegraph networks; operating a shipping service between Taiwan, Hong Kong and Fujian; establishing northern Taiwan's commercial center at Dadaocheng; revising rules for trade with the West; and building armory and machine manufacturing bureaus.

Liu's plans for development required financial support. Liu gained the required support, first, by conducting a land survey to ferret out land under cultivation that had not yet been subject to taxation, thereby increasing land tax revenues. Second, he sought the cooperation of Taiwan's landed gentry to secure investment in new government ventures. Liu, however, ended up ceding considerable economic rights to the gentry; the Lin family of Banciao and the Lin family of Wufong, for example, both received substantial exploitation and camphor rights.

Another notable policy of the Liu Mingchuan era was the aggressive campaign to "exploit the mountains and pacify the savages." With the development of the tea and camphor industries, Chinese settlers were increasingly encroaching into the mountain territory, creating hardships for the indigenous people. Moreover, Liu Mingchuan and Taiwan's gentry also waged frequent "pacification campaigns" to obtain the resources locked in the mountains.

【關鍵字】田賦 land tax revenues / 開山撫番 "exploit the mountains and pacify the savages"/
征番戰爭 "pacification campaigns"

台灣淪為日本的殖民地

　　一八九五年，大清帝國因為甲午戰爭失敗，與日本簽訂馬關條約，將台灣割讓給了日本。甲午戰爭原本是清國與日本為爭奪對朝鮮的主導權而爆發的戰爭，而且戰爭又都在北方展開，但是結果卻割讓台灣，使得台灣的士紳們都有被朝廷遺棄的感覺。交接之後，清朝在台的巡撫唐景崧與台灣北部士紳曾試圖成立一個沒有實質內容的「台灣民主國」來抵拒日本的領有，但不旋踵而終。反而是地區性的豪強所率領的自衛武力，以簡陋的武器與日本占領軍抗戰達四個月之久。

採取強硬手段統治台灣

　　日本一反清朝時代鬆散的統治方式，積極地企圖將其支配力貫徹到台灣社會的末端，並且積極介入社會的諸多事務，於是引發原本具有自治性質的台灣地方勢力的反撲。結果，日本殖民政府以武力威壓與利益誘發併用，拉攏上層、孤立強豪的分割統治手法，花費大約十年的時間，才完成島內的綏靖工作。

　　台灣雖然是日本帝國的新領土，但日本政府卻將台灣視為殖民地，在日本帝國憲法的架構之下，另外設計一套適用於台灣的法制體系。在這套法制體系當中，台灣總督府為台灣島內的最高行政機關，但卻沒有足以制衡它的議會。當然，台灣人

Taiwan Becomes a Japanese Colony

After the Sino-Japanese War in 1894-95, the defeated Cing Empire ceded Taiwan to Japan in the Treaty of Maguan (Treaty of Shimonoseki in Japanese). Although the Sino-Japanese War had initially erupted over a dispute between Japan and China regarding control over Korea and the war largely unfolded in the north, Taiwan was in the end ceded to Japan, leaving Taiwan's gentry feeling cast aside by the imperial court. Tang Jingsong, the Cing governor of Taiwan, and the gentry of northern Taiwan established their ineffectual "Taiwan Republic" to resist Japanese colonization, but it was not to last. Local strongmen, on the other hand, led a defense with rudimentary weapons and held out for four months against the Japanese.

Ruling Taiwan with an Iron Fist

The new Japanese rulers immediately set out to replace the loose Cing governing style with a rigid aggressive drive to impose their rule to the very roots of society. They became involved in various social affairs, provoking resistance among Taiwan's previously autonomous local power structure. The Japanese colonial government eventually used a combination of armed force and incentive to coax chosen members of the ruling class and isolate others. It took Japanese about 10 years to fully pacify Taiwan.

Although Taiwan became a part of the Japanese Empire, the government in Tokyo regarded Taiwan as a colony. Under the Japanese constitutional framework a separate legal system was established to apply specifically to Taiwan. Under this system, the

【關鍵字】中日甲午戰爭 the Sino-Japanese War / 馬關條約 the Treaty of Shimonoseki (Treaty of Maguan in Chinese) / 唐景崧巡撫 Governor Tang Jingsong/ 台灣民主國 Taiwan Republic / 日本殖民政府 the Japanese colonial government / 台灣總督府 the Taiwan Governor-General's Office

也沒有參政的機會，有的只是總督府為了攏絡士紳、地方名望家族而設的名譽職或服務性質的參事、庄長等職。

一九一九年，由於同是日本殖民地的朝鮮發生主張獨立的「三一獨立運動」，使日本政府將外地的統治政策改採「內地延長主義」，日本國內的各種政制才被施行於台灣。但仍加上各種限制，例如台灣仍無足以牽制行政機關的議會，而是由總督府自民間挑選任命一些人組成僅供諮詢的「評議會」。

發展殖民地生產事業

日本政府在台灣達成治安的掌握之後，也對台灣的投資生產環境進行改造。最主要的是統一度量衡、統一貨幣、確立土地所有權與進行交通建設、改善都市的環境衛生。確立土地所有權是進行土地調查，一方面掌握地籍做為課徵田賦的根據，一方面則收購傳統的大租權，認定小租主為近代意義的所有權人。交通建設，最主要的是建設島內的道路系統，興築縱貫鐵路與基隆港，使西部平原生產地帶有縱橫交錯的交通網，並透過縱貫鐵路聯結北部的基隆港。於是，台灣的產品可以透過這個交通網輸往日本。

日本資本在台灣的最大投資是製糖業。殖民政府以各種優惠扶持日本資本家在台設立大型的近代製糖廠。這種製糖業，由台灣農民種植製糖原料甘蔗，提供日本

Taiwan Governor-General's Office was the highest administrative authority in Taiwan, however, there was no representative assembly to balance the power of the executive. The Taiwanese, naturally, had almost no opportunity for political participation except where the colonial government sought to ingratiate themselves with local gentry or members of notable families by offering honorary or low-level service positions such as county counselor or village chief.

In 1919, the Korean colony launched the "First March Independence Movement" calling for independence from Japan, which prompted the Japanese Government to alter its policy towards external territories to one of "domestic expansionism." It was only then that many government systems that existed domestically in Japan were implemented in Taiwan, albeit with various restrictions. For example, Taiwan still had no representative assembly to serve as a balance to the administrative authority, but rather, an "Advisory Council" was picked by the colonial government to serve in a consultative capacity.

The Development of Colonial Enterprises

Once the Japanese Government had achieved social order in Taiwan, it set about improving the commercial investment climate. The most important initial tasks were the standardization of weights and measurements, the standardization of currency, verification of land title rights, construction of transport infrastructure and improvements to urban sanitation. To verify land rights a land survey was conducted, in part to firmly identify the landowners for tax collection purposes and in part to acquire large-rent and validate the recent claims of small-rent. The transportation construction projects included a network of roadways throughout the island. The north-to-south railroad connected the pro-

【關鍵字】三一獨立運動 the First March Independence Movement / 內地延長主義 domestic expansionism / 評議會 Advisory Council / 統一度量衡 the standardization of weights and measurements/ 日本資本家 Japanese capitalists

資本家所經營新式的製糖廠製糖，再將糖販運至日本國內市場。從生產到製造，再到市場的全部過程當中，日本政府都積極給予製糖產業各種政策性的配合，也因而讓製糖業成為日本在台灣最重要的殖民產業。

　　日本殖民政府不但積極地將其支配力滲透台灣華人的生息地帶，在一九一〇年代以後，也逐漸將行政力量伸進山區的原住民地區。早期，日本殖民政府以軍隊壓迫原住民，挺進「隘勇線」，確保淺山地區的樟腦生產地帶。接著沒收原住民槍械，試圖改變原住民的生活形態，教育原住民畜牧，甚至發展農業，使得原住民地域遭受到全面性的空前挑戰。

duction areas along the western plain with the Keelung Harbor. It was through this network that Taiwan's goods were shipped to Japan.

Japan's biggest investments in Taiwan were in sugar production. The colonial government provided various preferential measures for Japanese enterprises to set up modern sugar refineries in Taiwan. Taiwanese farmers would provide raw sugar cane to sugar refineries operated by Japanese capitalists who would then make sugar for export to the home Japanese market. Japanese government policy actively gave assistance to sugar producers at every step of the process from cultivation and refining to the marketplace, making sugar refining Japan's most important colonial enterprise in Taiwan.

The Japanese colonial government not only actively sought to extend its control over areas settled by the Chinese, but in the period following 1910 it began to gradually extend its administrative influence into mountain areas controlled by indigenous tribes. At the beginning, the Japanese colonial government used military units to suppress the indigenous peoples and establish a defensive perimeter around the camphor production regions in the foothills. After confiscating indigenous peoples' weapons, the Japanese embarked upon a scheme to change the lifestyle of the tribes, teaching them to raise animals and helping them develop agriculture. Indigenous peoples were now facing an unprecedented challenge to their way of life.

【關鍵字】隘勇線 defensive perimeter

台灣人開始覺醒

　　第一次大戰前後，國際上的殖民地統治逐漸走向自治主義，日本國內也正是比較開放的「大正民主時代」。一九一九年，與台灣同樣是日本殖民地的朝鮮爆發「三一獨立運動」，使原本便主張「內地延長主義」的原敬總理大臣，迅速調整「外地」統治政策。從此以後，對台灣的統治，名義上施用與日本相同的制度與法律，但卻仍有不少因為台灣的特殊情況而特別施政者。

台灣人要求提高自主權

　　就在國際上、日本國內的氣氛變動之際，日本的台灣殖民地統治原則也在漸漸鬆動，台灣第一代近代知識份子正好在此時刻長成。這些人出生於一八九五年日本統治之後，從小接受日本所導入的新式教育，由於大多出身台灣的地主富裕家庭，有能力接受高等教育，甚至不少還留學日本。他們不但受到各種近代思潮的洗禮，而且年輕具有改革的理想與熱情。於是，在時潮的鼓舞與日本政府所提供的合法空間內，於一九二〇年代展開了一場文化啟蒙運動與政治社會運動。

　　一九二一年起至一九三四年，前後持續十五次的「台灣議會設置請願運動」是最重要的參政權要求運動。此運動的理論根據是，既然日本是個民主憲政國家，台

The Awakening of the Taiwan People

During the time just before and after World War I, colonial powers increasingly permitted autonomy among their colonies. At the same time, Japan was experiencing a period of openness known as the Taisho Democracy Era, and on March 1, 1919, an event known as the "First March Independence Movement" occurred in Korea, a country that like Taiwan, was under Japanese control. This prompted Prime Minister Hara Takashi, who had originally advocated a policy of bringing its colonies within the Japanese system, to adjust Japan's policies with respect to its governance of what would be considered as "foreign territory." Although in name the systems and laws applied in Taiwan were supposed to be the same as those in Japan, there remained many exceptions due to Taiwan's "special circumstances."

The Taiwanese Demand Greater Autonomy

It was also during this time of change around the world and in Japan that Taiwan's first generation of modern intellectuals emerged. Born in Taiwan subsequent to the Japanese colonization in 1895, these intellectuals received a Japanese education from childhood. Most of them came from relatively well-to-do families of the landlord or gentry class, and thus attained a high level of education in Taiwan and in many cases pursued advanced study in Japan. They were exposed to different schools of contemporary thought, were full of idealism, and enthusiastically supported reform. Riding on the momentum of reform and taking advantage of the relatively liberal laws and policies of the Japanese Government at the time, these Taiwanese intellectuals were the vanguard of Taiwan's social, political and cultural enlightenment movements in the 1920s.

【關鍵字】大正民主時代 the Taisho Democracy Era / 文化啟蒙運動 the cultural enlightenment movements /
台灣議會設置請願運動 the Taiwan Representative Assembly Petition Movement

灣又是日本帝國之領土，自然也必須實行民主憲政，因此台灣應該有民主憲政所必須的議會。運動的方式，則是根據日本帝國憲法賦予人民的請願權，於每年以簽名請願的方式向帝國議會提出請願書。因此，這個運動算是非常穩健的合法運動，但日本政府卻以若允許設置台灣議會，將會成為是給予台灣自治的第一步，而始終未允許台灣人的要求。

　　與台灣議會設置請願運動大約同時展開的，還有以提升台灣文化水準為目的的文化啟蒙團體「台灣文化協會」的活動。台灣文化協會透過演講、發行報刊、舉辦研習營等方式，宣揚近代的各種思想，企圖打破傳統的固陋思想，革除迷信。

　　台灣文化協會與議會設置請願運動展開之後，台灣人的運動逐漸升高訴求。一九二八年，蔣渭水組織了主張自治的政黨「台灣民眾黨」。還有以從事農民運動為目標的「農民組合」，甚至有非法的「台灣共產黨」。但是，這些政黨尚無法充分發揮，只能從事政治宣傳，而且進入一九三○年代以後，也先後被日本殖民政府所禁止。

米糖經濟發展至高峰

　　第一次世界大戰，不但使台灣糖得以趁機輸入歐洲市場，造成台灣糖業的更進一步發展；而且日本也因偏重工商業發展而發生缺糧現象。於是，一九二○年代日

The Taiwan Representative Assembly Petition Movement was the most important movement in Taiwan for asserting the right to participate in the government. Carried out from 1921 to 1934, the theoretical foundation of the movement was based on the assertion that since Japan was a constitutional democracy, Taiwan, as a part of the Japanese Empire, should have a democratic government and council as well. Every year during this period petitions were submitted to the Japanese Imperial Diet. This movement became well established and was fully in accordance with the existing laws and regulations of the time. While the Japanese allowed the establishment of a number of councils and committees, the requests of the Representative Assembly Petition Movement were denied for fear that acceptance might be the first step in Taiwan's achieving autonomy.

A movement to elevate Taiwan culture led by the Taiwan Culture Association (TCA) was initiated at roughly the same time as the Taiwan Representative Assembly Petition Movement. The TCA held speeches, published periodicals and offered training courses promoting modern ideas and programs with the hope of ridding Taiwan society of traditional beliefs that were thought to be a hindrance to modernization.

The aims sought in the efforts that followed were even more ambitious. In 1928, the pro-autonomy Taiwan People's Party was established by Jiang Weishuei. At the same time groups such as the Farmers' Association, whose objective was to lead farmers movements, and even an illegal Taiwan Communist Party were formed. Although these groups never fully realized their potential, they did engage in extensive activities to educate the public on their principles and goals. In the 1930s the Japanese colonial government clamped down and the number of opposition activists sharply declined.

【關鍵字】民主憲政 constitutional democracy / 台灣文化協會 the Taiwan Culture Association (TCA) /
台灣民眾黨 Taiwan People's Party / 蔣渭水 Jiang Weishuei / 農民組合 Farmers' Association / 台灣共產黨
Taiwan Communist Party

本政府在台灣鼓勵增產以輸出日本市場為目的的蓬萊米。從此，米、糖成為「農業台灣」供應「工業日本」的兩項重要產品，這也促使日本願意在台灣從事農田水利灌溉、品種改良、農業加工技術研究等投資，因此有所謂日本在台灣從事了一次「綠色革命」的說法。

一九三〇年代起，由於日本軍國主義法西斯的抬頭，台灣總督府一方面在農村培養新世代的領導者，一方面配合其南進國策，調整台灣的產業。除了在農業方面強調多樣化之外，並在台灣推動工業化，使日本內地、台灣、南洋形成產業的垂直互補關係，使得台灣在極短的期間內工業生產量快速攀升，但不久便因戰爭而停頓。

一九三〇年代末期，台灣也被編組在日本的戰時體制之內，不但生產要提供戰爭所用，勞力也被以「奉公」的名義動員投入各種戰時工程建設。日本政府為確保台灣人支持其戰爭，還發動「皇民化運動」，企圖使台灣人成為效忠於天皇的「皇民」，最後甚至徵調台灣人服兵役，投入戰場。

The Kings of Taiwan's Economy: Rice and Sugar

One effect of World War I was that the Taiwan sugar industry received a boost when sugar began to be exported to Europe. Also due to the war, Japan experienced a grain shortage at home since a priority had been placed on industrial development. In response, during the 1920s, the Japanese Government encouraged production of rice in Taiwan. Rice and sugar became two important products for "agricultural Taiwan" to supply "industrial Japan." Japan was thus willing to invest in irrigation, strain improvement, and processing technology in Taiwan. The combination of these activities would become known as Japan's "green revolution" in Taiwan.

Beginning in the 1930s, with the rise of Japanese militarism and fascism, the Taiwan Governor-General's Office cultivated a new generation of leaders in rural areas and, in line with it's national policy of southern advancement, made adjustments to Taiwan's industries. It encouraged agricultural diversification and implemented industrialization in Taiwan. These measures forged a linear complimentary relationship among Japan, Taiwan, and areas of the south Pacific. Taiwan's industrial production accelerated rapidly during these years, only to be slowed down as Japan's military efforts increased and the country's attention was focused on the war.

Toward the end of the 1930s, Taiwan was mobilized to support the Japanese war machine. Taiwanese production and labor were pressed into wartime service "in tribute" to the Empire. In an effort to shore up support from the Taiwanese, Japan launched the the Kominka Movement with the express purpose of transforming the Taiwanese into loyal subjects of the Empire. Ultimately Taiwanese were drafted for military service and some fought on the front lines and lost their lives for the Japanese.

【關鍵字】日本軍國主義法西斯 Japanese militarism and fascism / 奉公 in tribute /
皇民化運動 the Kominka Movement (literally, the Japanization Movenent)

戰後的威權體制國家

一九四五年八月十五日，日本宣布投降。十月二十五日，中國政府派陳儀來台接受日軍的投降，並著手接收工作。

戰爭結束使台灣人終於可以乍見曙光，遺憾的是，雖然台灣人對未來充滿憧憬與期待，但是陳儀的接收政府卻使台灣人失望了。

期待的落空與無奈

在經濟方面，中國政府的接收官員多半貪污腐敗，不少人將公家財產納入私囊，而且也沒有能力經營接收成為公營的各種生產事業，造成生產停頓、失業嚴重。在政治方面，來自中國的「外省人」如同日本人，占據了日本殖民者離去後的高層，台灣人仍然只能擔任低層的職位，甚至以不會說「國語」的理由，被排除就任公職的機會。台灣人的處境並未因殖民統治結束而有所改善。

一九四七年二月二十七日，台北大稻埕發生一起警民衝突事件，警察誤殺一名市民，翌日（二十八日）台北市發生示威遊行抗議，但卻遭警察以機關槍掃射。於

The Post-War Autocracy

Japan announced its surrender on 15 August 1945 and, subsequently, on 25 October of the same year, the Chinese government dispatched Fujian Governor Chen Yi to accept the Japanese surrender and begin the process of taking over the management of Taiwan.

The people of Taiwan greeted the end of the war with high hopes and aspirations for the future. Chen Yi's new government, unfortunately, soon turned these hopes into disappointment and bitterness.

Dashed Hopes

Economically, the change in rule was disastrous. The Chinese officials dispatched to Taiwan were corrupt and many of them appropriated public property for their private fortunes. Moreover, they lacked the ability to manage the enterprises that were taken over as state-owned businesses and, as a result, production dropped, unemployment soared and the island's economy was soon in crisis. In politics, high-level positions once occupied by the Japanese were soon filled with "mainlanders" (people from "mainland China"). Consequently, Taiwanese could still only hold low-level positions and many were denied access to public service jobs due to their inability to speak the "national language," Mandarin, which is largely based on the language used in the area around Beijing. As a result, there was little improvement in the status of the Taiwanese in the post-war period.

On February 27, 1947, a confrontation between Taiwanese citizens and mainlander police in Dadaocheng, Taipei, ended in the accidental killing of a bystander. The follow-

【關鍵字】福建省長陳儀 Fujian Governor Chen Yi / 示威抗議遊行 demonstration

是，暴動迅速蔓延全島。當時的最高主管機關「台灣行政長官公署」無法控制局面，藉由民意代表及台灣各界領導者組成「二二八事件處理委員會」，安撫民心。處委會趁機提出改革台灣政治的多項建議，長官公署為求穩住情勢，拖延時間，一方面口頭應允處委會的要求，一方面卻暗中向南京的中央政府要求派兵鎮壓。三月八日，大陸援軍抵達台灣，隨即展開「無差別」的報復性屠殺，並且在事件後以「清鄉」名義搜索「叛黨」，估計數月間，台灣人遭害者達兩萬人以上，其中包括眾多的各界菁英。

一九四九年底，在國共內戰中失利的國民黨政府退來台灣，雖然一時情況頗為危急，但卻因翌年（一九五〇年）六月韓戰的爆發，使美國介入台灣海峽，甚至於一九五一年二月與中華民國簽訂軍事援助協定。台灣成為美國等西方資本主義陣營在東亞防堵社會主義陣營的一個重要環節。從此以後，「國共內戰」在「美蘇冷戰」的結構中被凍結了下來。

製造強固的獨裁政權

美蘇對立下，台灣成為東亞冷戰的前線，國民黨政府得以獲得美國之軍事保護，而有喘息的餘裕。於是，蔣介石趁機在台灣從事國民黨的「改造」，不但整頓與改變黨的組織，而且瓦解黨內派閥，貫徹「領袖獨裁」，以黨對國家機構進行一元化之指導，重建「以黨領政」、「以黨領軍」為精神的政黨國家。另外，在加強

ing day, February 28, the incident escalated when police responded to demonstrations in Taipei with machine-gun fire. As a result, riots quickly spread throughout the island. When the Taiwan Governor-General's Office (the highest government office at the time) was unable to quell the turmoil, a special commission comprising public representatives and various community leaders attempted to bring about the Committee for Settling February 28 Incident. The commission took advantage of the opportunity to present numerous recommendations for political reform. The Governor-General's Office, in an effort to calm the situation, stalled for time by consenting to the commission's demands. What the commission did not know, however, was that the Governor-General's office had secretly sent a request to the central government in Nanking to dispatch troops to "quell the insurrection." Chinese troops arrived on March 8 and began a campaign of retaliation. People were indiscriminately slaughtered and information was collected on other "insurgents" under the name of "purifying the countryside." Over twenty thousand Taiwanese were killed during campaign and the lives of many of Taiwan's most talented youth were lost.

By the end of 1949, the KMT Government was facing imminent defeat by the Chinese Communists. However, when the Korean War broke out in June 1950 following the Nationalist retreat to Taiwan, the U.S. stepped in and Taiwan found itself to be a "strategic" link in the Asian anti-communist defense chain. This sparked the signing of a U.S./Taiwan Mutual Defense Treaty in February 1951 and, as a result, the standoff between the KMT and the Communist regime became intertwined with the cold war between the United States and the Soviet Union.

【關鍵字】台灣行政長官公署 Taiwan Governor-General's Office / 二二八事件處理委員會 the Committee for Settling February 28 Incident / 清鄉 purifying the countryside / 國民黨 the KMT (also known as Kuomintang or Chinese Nationalist Party) / 中華民國 the Republic of China (R.O.C) / 中美軍事防禦協定 U.S. Taiwan Mutual Defense Treaty / 冷戰 the cold war / 蔣介石 Chiang Kaishek

社會控制方面，則發布「戒嚴令」實施軍事管制，而且配合情治特務系統，嚴密監控可能的反對勢力。接著又以「動員戡亂時期臨時條款」，一方面強化總統的權力，一方面將憲法所規範的憲政「空洞化」。

戰後的台灣經濟，除了須進行戰災復興，還要供養一九四九年短期間大量湧入的軍公教消費人口，又要負擔國共軍事對抗的龐大軍費，可謂極端艱困。在一九六五年之前，美國的經濟支援確實適度發揮了補貼的作用；更值得注意的是，日本時代所留下的各項基本建設（如交通、電力、人才等）和已有相當基礎的農林產業，配合台灣人全體的辛勞勤奮，才是度過此艱困的重要憑藉。

Creating a Powerful Dictatorship

Having become one of the front lines in the Soviet-U.S. struggle, the KMT Government gained some breathing space under U.S. military protection. Chiang Kai-shek, chairman of the KMT, seized upon this opportunity to "reform" the party, which meant not only reorganizing and reforming party structure, but also breaking down internal factions in order to consolidate power. He unified all political and military power under the party and Taiwan became, in essence a party-state. Furthermore, in order to strengthen social control, martial law was declared and a network of secret agents and informers was set up to closely monitor any potential opposition. In addition, the enforcement of the "Articles of National Mobilization for the Suppression of the Communist Rebellion," also enabled Chiang to suspend constitutional rights and enhance the powers of the president.

In addition to recovering from the war, Taiwan's economy was forced to support some two million newcomers from China that came arrived the Chinese Communist's victories in 1949, as well as absorbing the huge costs of supporting the KMT's anti-Communist military campaign. While U.S. aid through 1965 helped sustain Taiwan, it should also be noted that the solid and extensive infrastructure left by the Japanese (transportation, utilities and an educated population) along with the resolve of the Taiwanese people were of great importance in these very troubled times.

【關鍵字】戒嚴令 martial law / 情治特務系統 network of secret agents and informers /
動員勘亂時期臨時條款 the Articles of National Mobilization for the Suppression of the Communist Rebellion

邁向政治民主化之路

　　隨著社會主義陣營的中（共）蘇對立擴大，東西冷戰結構逐漸崩解，美國也有意拉攏中共牽制蘇聯。於是，中華民國在國際上的處境日益困難，尤其是一九七一年失去聯合國的席次之後，便接二連三與世界主要國家陸續斷交。

開放參政空間

　　在國際處境困難的同時，也正是蔣介石年事已高，蔣經國實質掌握國家最高權力的時候。蔣經國一方面以「十大建設」挽回傾向逃避（移民、資本外流）的人心，一方面洞悉知識份子亟望改革的要求，實行政治改革。以國會議員的增補選、任用本省籍青年才俊的方式，適度吸納民意，並補充逐漸凋謝的「法統」。

　　一九六九年，從未改選的國會，進行小幅度的「增補選」；一九七二年起又有定期改選的「增額選舉」。此項「增額選舉」，一方面得以利用選舉補充逐漸消滅的「法統」，另一方面因為只是針對少數「增額議員」進行選舉，故國民黨即使選舉結果失敗，也不虞喪失國會中的絕對優勢。如此聊勝於無的選舉，卻得以逐漸開啟台灣人制度性的國政參與空間。從此以後，台灣也有了比較具有組織的政治對抗者，

The Path to Democracy

During the 1970s, relations between the Soviet Union and China worsened while the cold war between the United States and the U.S.S.R. began to thaw. This spelled danger for Taiwan as the U.S. saw an opportunity to gain leverage over the U.S.S.R. by establishing friendly relations with China. Taiwan's precarious position in the international political arena grew even more serious following the Republic of China's loss of her seat at the U.N. in 1972, and the continued severance of formal relations with the R.O.C. by nearly all of Taiwan's former allies.

Small Openings for Political Participation

This diplomatic predicament and the advanced age of President Chiang Kai-shek were the important background against which Chiang's elder son, Chiang Ching-kuo, consolidated his succession to power. He took two measures that would prove instrumental in turning around the nation's fortunes. First, he initiated the "Ten Major Construction Projects" in a bid to secure people's confidence and stem the emigration and flow of capital from the country. Second, he implemented some political reforms in response to calls from intellectuals. Through the holding of supplementary elections for the National Assembly and Legislative Yuan, and by his appointment of young Taiwanese talent to government positions, he was able to gain a measure of goodwill. He was also able to bolster somewhat the orthodoxy of the R.O.C. that had already begun to wither away.

For the first time ever supplemental elections were held in 1969 for a handful of National Assembly seats. Starting in 1972, elections for additional seats in the Legislative Yuan were held regularly. Ironically these elections served to shore up the KMT rule, for on the one hand, the elections gave an appearance of democracy, while at the same time only a few seats were at stake so there was be no real threat to the KMT's absolute dominance even if non-KMT people were elected. So while little of substance was changed by the elections, they were landmarks for the political participation of native Taiwanese. It was at this time that Taiwan saw the formation of an organized political opposition, the Dangwai, a term that literally means "outsiders of the KMT."

【關鍵字】中共（中華人民共和國）the People's Republic of China (P.R.C.) / 蔣經國 Chiang Ching-kuo / 十大建設 Ten Major Construction Projects / 國民大會 the National Assembly / 立法院 the Legislative Yuan / 法統 orthodoxy of the R.O.C.

即「黨外」。

「黨外」人士的積極爭取

一九七九年，集結多數「黨外」人士的《美麗島》雜誌創刊，獲得民眾的廣泛支持，而快速發展成具有準政黨的態勢。但是，該年底發生「高雄事件」，國民黨情治系統（通稱「鷹派」）勢力藉此事件反撲，不但大量逮捕「黨外」，並引發「林宅血案」，造成國內外之反感。此後，一九八一年的「陳文成事件」、一九八四年的「江南事件」，均被認為與國民黨鷹派有關。不過，這些事件不但未使反對勢力退縮，反而增加同仇敵愾之心，甚至招致美國國會及國際人權保護組織的關切，使國民黨被迫更加放寬自由的空間。

一九八六年，「黨外」進一步正式組織「民主進步黨」；蔣經國主政的國民黨除默認之外，翌年（一九八七年）並解除長達三十八年的戒嚴。一九八八年初，蔣經國逝世，李登輝繼任總統。

一九九〇年代以後，李登輝一方面宣布終止「動員戡亂時期」，結束與中國的內戰態勢，並且尋求兩岸間的和平對話；另一方面進行國民大會及立法院的全面改選，使國會真正能夠代表台灣，並逐漸修改憲法，進行憲政改革。

Dangwai Demands for More Political Participation

1979 saw the publication of the first edition of the Formosa Magazine. Published by a group of Dangwai members, the magazine was very well received by the public. This and other successes soon lifted the Dangwai's position to that of a political party in waiting. However, this momentum terminated abruptly in December of the same year with the occurrence of the Kaohsiung Incident. A group of hardliners within the KMT's intelligence system (known in the Chinese language by the word for "hawk") were far less tolerant of the reforms and launched a large-scale suppression campaign against the fledgling democracy movement. The action led to the arrests of many Dangwai leaders and other members, as well as the shocking massacre of Lin Yi-syong's family. The subsequent murder of Chen Wen-cheng and Jiang Nan, both of which were alleged to have connections to the KMT's hawks, stunned people at home and around the world. Undeterred, the Dangwai and other opposition supporters stuck together and fought even harder to achieve their common goals of freedom and democracy. Even the U.S. Congress and international human rights organizations expressed concern, and this combination of local resolve and foreign pressure forced the KMT Government to further loosen control.

The Dangwai formally established itself as the Democratic Progressive Party (DPP) in 1986. The KMT, then headed by Chiang Ching-kuo, accepted the party (although technically it was still illegal to establish political parties), and the next year President Chiang Ching-kuo ordered that the 38-year martial law legacy of his father be lifted. Chiang Ching-kuo passed away in 1988 and was succeeded by his Vice President, Li Teng-hui.

Throughout the nineties President Li completed a number of major reforms. He ended "the Period of Mobilization to Suppress the Communist Rebellion" thus terminating the state of "civil war" between Taiwan and China, and he began a peaceful dialog with China after nearly fifty years of no formal communication with communist government of China. He brought about full elections in the National Assembly and the Legislative Yuan as well as direct presidential elections thus enabling the people of Taiwan to have a true voice in government. He also began the long and arduous task of constitutional reform by initiating a series of amendments to the Constitution.

【關鍵字】黨外 "outsiders of the KMT" / 美麗島雜誌 the Formosa Magazine / 高雄事件 the Kaohsiung Incident / 林義雄宅血案 the massacre of Lin Yi-syong's family / 陳文成事件 the murder of Chen Wen-cheng Incident / 江南案 the murder of Jiang Nan / 民主進步黨 the Democratic Progressive Party (DPP) / 李登輝 Li Teng-hui

【台灣歷史年表】
Taiwan Timeline

縱貫上萬年的歷史年表，台灣大小事一覽無遺！

The major events of Taiwan's history can be seen at a glance in these timelines spanning thousands of years.

史前遺跡時間分布	舊石器時代晚期 （距今一五〇〇〇年至 五〇〇〇年前）	長濱文化 （主要分布在台灣東部及 恆春半島海岸）	
	新石器時代早期 （距今七〇〇〇年至 五〇〇〇年前）	大坌坑文化 （遍布全台）	
	新石器時代中期 （距今五〇〇〇年至 三五〇〇？年前）	圓山文化 （主要分布於 新店溪、淡水河階及 台北盆地邊緣）	
	新石器時代晚期 （距今三五〇〇？年至 二〇〇〇年前）	芝山岩文化	 圓山文化晚期 植物園文化 土地公山系統文化 營埔文化
	金屬器時代 （距今約二五〇〇年至 四〇〇年前）	十三行文化 （遍布台北、宜蘭、 桃竹苗地區）	

Relics of Pre-History	Late Paleolithic Period: From 15,000 to 5,000 years ago	**Changbin Culture** Mostly scattered across coastal areas of eastern Taiwan and the Hengchun Peninsula	
	Early Neolithic Period: From 7,000 to 5,000 years ago	**Dabenkeng Culture** Throughout Taiwan	
	Middle Neolithic Period: From 5,000 to about 3,500? years ago	**Yuanshan Culture** Located mostly around the Sindian River, Danshuei River areas and the edges of the Taipei Basin	
	Late Neolithic Period: From 3,500? to 2,000 years ago	**Jhihshihyan Culture**	Late Yuanshan Culture Botanical Garden Culture Tudigongshan Culture Yingpu Culture
	Iron Age: From 2,500 to 400 years ago	**Shihsanhang Culture** Scattered across Taipei, Yilan, Taoyuan, Hsinchu and Miaoli counties	

網形文化
（主要分布於西海岸中北部
丘陵台地區）

老崩山系統文化

牛罵頭文化
（主要分布於台中、南投一帶）

牛稠子文化

繩紋紅陶文化
（主要分布於東海岸）

大湖文化

鳳鼻頭文化

卑南文化
（分布於花東地區）

大坑文化
（分布於花蓮縣壽豐鄉）

麒麟文化
（分布於東海岸）

番仔園文化
（主要分布於
中部沿海）

大邱園文化
（分布於濁水溪中游）

蔦松文化
（主要分布於台南、
高雄平原）

北葉文化

龜山文化

靜浦文化

Wangsing Culture
Mostly scattered across terraced hillside areas in northern and central areas of west coast Taiwan.

Laobengshan Culture

Nioumatou Culture
Located mostly in the Taichung, Nantou region

Niouchouzih Culture

Eastern Rope Pattern Terracotta Culture
Located mostly along the east coast

Dahu Culture

Fongbitou Culture

Puyuma Culture
Located in the Hualien-Taitung region

Dakeng Culture
Shoufong Township, Hualien County

Cilin Culture
East coast

Fanzaiyuan Culture
Mostly located in the central coastal areas

Daciouyuan Culture
Located along the middle reaches of the Jhuoshuei River

Niaosong Culture
Mostly located on the plains in Kaohsiung and Tainan

Beiye Culture

Guishan Culture

Jingpu Culture

年代		台灣大事記
一五四四年	明世宗嘉靖二十三年	◎葡萄牙人航經台灣，稱台灣為美麗島（Ilha Formosa）。
一六〇三年至一六〇四年	明神宗萬曆三十二年	◎荷蘭人韋麻郎（Wijbrand van Waerwijck）率領船艦到澎湖，要求和中國貿易。
一六二四年	明熹宗天啟四年	◎占據澎湖的荷蘭人遭到明朝守將俞咨皋逼退，轉而進據台灣，在今台南安平一帶登陸。
一六二五年	天啟五年	◎荷蘭人購買新港社的赤崁地方，建造普羅民遮城（Provintia）。
一六二六年	天啟六年	◎西班牙人攻占雞籠，在今基隆和平島建聖救主城（St. Salvador）。
一六二七年	天啟七年	◎荷蘭牧師康德（Georgius Candiduis）到新港社（今台南一帶）傳教。
一六二八年	明思宗崇禎元年	◎西班牙人在淡水傳教。 ◎日本人濱田彌兵衛俘虜荷蘭長官奴易茲（Pieter Nuyts）。
一六三〇年	崇禎三年	◎荷蘭派兵鎮壓新港社。
一六三二年	崇禎五年	◎西班牙人溯淡水河，進入台北盆地。

Year (Western / Imperial calendars)		Major events in Taiwan
1544	The 23rd year of the Jiajing reign period of Ming Emperor Shihzong	◎Portuguese ships sail by Taiwan. The Portuguese name Taiwan Ihla Formosa (Beautiful Island).
1603-1604	The 32rd year of the Wanli reign period of Ming Emperor Shenzong	◎Dutchman Wijbrand van Waerwijck sails to Penghu to establish trade relations with China.
1624	The 4th year of the Tianic reign period of Ming Emperor Sizong	◎The Dutch move to Taiwan, landing in what is modern day Anping, Tainan, after the Ming navy drives them from Penghu.
1625	Tianci Year 5	◎The Dutch build Fort Provintia on land known as Sakkam purchased from Sinkan Village (now Tainan).
1626	TianciYear 6	◎Spaniards occupy Keelung and establish San Salvador on what is now called Hoping Island.
1627	Tianci Year 7	◎Dutch missionary Reverend Georgius Candidus arrives at Sinkan Village.
1628	The first year of the Chongjhen reign period of Ming Emperor Sihzong	◎The Spaniards set up a Catholic mission in Danshuei. ◎The Japanese businessman Hamado Yahyoe captures the Dutch Governor-General Pieter Nuyts.
1630	Chongjhen Year 3	◎The Dutch sends a military force to put down the revolt at Sinkan Village.
1632	Chongjhen Year 5	◎The Spaniards find their way to the Taipei Basin by following the Danshuei River upstream.

年代		台灣大事記
一六三六年	崇禎九年	◎荷蘭人征服了從不順服的麻豆（今台南麻豆）、蕭壠（今台南佳里）等社。 ◎台灣南部平埔族二十八社代表集合於新港社，向荷蘭聯合東印度公司宣示效忠。 ◎淡水的原住民反抗西班牙人。
一六四二年	崇禎十五年	◎西班牙人被荷蘭逼出台灣北部。
一六四五年	清世祖順治二年	◎荷蘭人第一次召集平埔族長老，成立「評議會」。
一六五二年	順治九年	◎華人郭懷一率眾反抗荷蘭人失敗，其部下約四千人被殺，另有一千多名華人遭株連。
一六六一年	順治十八年	◎鄭成功進攻澎湖，並從台南鹿耳門登陸台灣。
一六六二年	清聖祖康熙元年	◎荷蘭人投降，結束在台灣三十八年的統治。

Year (Western / Imperial calendars)		Major events in Taiwan
1636	Chongjhen Year 9	◎The Dutch put down resistance in Mattau(now Madou, Tainan) and Soulong (now Jiali, Tainan). ◎Representatives from 28 of southern Taiwan's plains indigenous villages gather at Sinkan swear an oath of loyalty to the Dutch East India Company. ◎Indigenous people in Danshuei revolt against the Spaniards.
1642	Chongjhen Year 15	◎The Dutch expel the Spaniards from northern Taiwan.
1645	The 2nd year of the Shunjhih reign period of Cing Emperor Shihzu	◎The Dutch first call on plains indigenous elders to form a Consultative Council.
1652	Shihzu Year 9	◎A rebellion against the Dutch led by Chinese Guo Huaiyi fails. About 4,000 rebels are massacred and more than 1,000 are taken prisoner.
1661	Shihzu Year 18	◎Jheng Chenggong (also known as Koxinga) attacks Penghu and then lands in Luermen, Tainan.
1662	The first year of the Kangsi reign period of Cing Emperor Shengzu	◎The Dutch surrender Taiwan to Jheng Chenggong, ending 38 years of occupation.

年代		台灣大事記
一六二八年	明思宗崇禎元年	◎鄭芝龍接受明朝招撫。
一六四四年	清世祖順治元年	◎李自成攻陷北京，崇禎皇帝自殺。 ◎鄭芝龍支持福王成立南明抗清政權。
一六四五年	清聖祖順治二年	◎唐王賜鄭成功朱姓，人稱「國姓爺」。
一六四六年	順治三年	◎鄭芝龍投降清朝。鄭成功棄文從武，領兵作戰。
一六五九年	順治十六年	◎鄭成功聯合張煌言攻打長江流域失敗。
一六六一年	順治十八年	◎鄭成功進攻澎湖，並從台南鹿耳門登陸台灣。 ◎鄭成功的部下到台灣各地「屯田」。 ◎鄭成功以台灣為「東都」，設置承天府（赤崁）及天興、萬年二縣。
一六六二年	清聖祖康熙元年	◎鄭成功病死。 ◎鄭經從廈門到台灣繼承鄭成功之位。
一六六三年	康熙二年	◎荷蘭、清軍聯手攻打金門、廈門，鄭經退守銅山。

Year (Western / Imperial calendars)		Major events in Taiwan
1628	The first year of the reign period of Chongjhen of Ming Emperor Sihzong	◎Jheng Jhihlong accepts the patronage of the Ming Dynasty.
1644	The first year of the reign period of Shunjhih of Cing Emperor Shihzu	◎Li Zihcheng invades Beijing; the Ming Emperor Sihzong hangs himself. ◎Jheng Jhihlong supports King Fu's organization of the Southern Ming court to challenge the Manchu regime.
1645	Shunjhih Year 2	◎King Tang bestows the royal name on Jheng Chenggong, who was thereafter called Koxinga (literally means "the Lord with the royal name").
1647	Shunjhih Year 4	◎Jheng Jhihlong surrenders to the Manchu; Jheng Chenggong abandons academia for military pursuits and leads troops into battle.
1659	Shunjhih Year 16	◎Jheng Chenggong allies himself with Jhang Huangyan in a Yangtze delta campaign and is defeated.
1661	Shunjhih Year 18	◎Jheng Chenggong seizes Penghu and later lands at Luermen near modern-day Tainan. ◎Jheng forces institute military settlement farming system. ◎Jheng declares Taiwan the Eastern Capital of the Ming Government and establishes an administration center, the Chengtian Fu (formerly Fort Provintia), and two counties, Tiansing and Wannian.
1662	The first year of the Kangsi Period of Cing Emperor Shengzu	◎Jheng Chenggong dies of illness. ◎Jheng Jing arrives in Taiwan from Siamen to inherit the position of Jheng Chenggong.
1663	Kangsi Year 2	◎The Dutch ally with Cing forces to attack Kinmen and Siamen. Jheng Jing retreats to Tongshan.

年代		台灣大事記
一六六四年	康熙三年	◎鄭氏改稱東都為東寧，天興、萬年縣改為「州」。 ◎鄭經放棄金門、廈門。
一六六五年	康熙四年	◎陳永華教民眾曬鹽，並制定「保甲制度」。
一六六六年	康熙五年	◎陳永華建議建孔廟、設學校。
一六七〇年	康熙九年	◎鄭氏部將劉國軒鎮壓沙轆原住民，數百人遭殺戮殆盡，只餘六人 　潛匿海口。
一六七三年	康熙十二年	◎中國發生三藩之亂。鄭經進兵大陸。
一六八一年	康熙二十年	◎鄭經去世。鄭克塽繼位。
一六八三年	康熙二十二年	◎施琅率清軍攻打澎湖、台灣，鄭軍不敵。 ◎鄭克塽投降。
一六八四年	康熙二十三年	◎台灣被劃歸清帝國的版圖，設台灣府，隸屬於福建省。

Year (Western / Imperial calendars)		Major events in Taiwan
1664	Kangsi Year 3	◎The Jheng clan changes the name of the Eastern Capital to Dongning; Tiansing and Wannian counties are reclassified "subprefecture." ◎Jheng Jing abandons Kinmen and Siamen.
1665	Kangsi Year 4	◎Chen Yonghua instructs the people on salt production and institutes the "bao-jia" system.
1666	Kangsi Year 5	◎Chen Yonghua advocates establishment of a Confucian temple and school.
1670	Kangsi Year 9	◎General Liu Guosyuan massacres several hundred indigenous peoples at Shalu, killing several hundred; only six survivors escape to the coast.
1673	Kangsi Year 12	◎The Revolt of the Three Feudatories breaks out in China; Jheng Jing joins the revolt.
1681	Kangsi Year 20	◎Jheng Jing dies; Jheng Keshuang assumes the throne.
1683	Kangsi Year 22	◎Shih Lang leads Cing troops in assault on Penghu and Taiwan; Jheng forces were no match. ◎Jheng Keshuang surrenders.
1684	Kangsi Year 23	◎Taiwan is included in the Cing Empire administrative system; establishing "Taiwan Prefecture" as a part of Fujian Province.

年代		台灣大事記
一六八四年	清聖祖康熙二十三年	◎建台灣府學及台灣、鳳山縣學。
一六八六年	康熙二十五年	◎客家人至下淡水平原（今日屏東）開墾。
一六九四年	康熙三十三年	◎知府高拱乾編修《台灣府志》。
一六九七年	康熙三十六年	◎郁永河至北部採硫磺，一六九八年寫成《裨海紀遊》。
一六九九年	康熙三十八年	◎吞霄社原住民反抗通事暴虐；淡水、北投社反抗。
一七○九年	康熙四十八年	◎陳賴章拓墾大佳臘（今台北市西園）。
一七一一年	康熙五十年	◎清朝政府規定：凡是從內地（大陸）來台灣的人，必須在原籍地開具證明，並在期限內回去。
一七一四年	康熙五十三年	◎清朝政府規定：人民到大甲溪以北之處，必須得到官府允許；淡水地區被認為是不文明的「化外之地」。
一七一六年	康熙五十五年	◎岸裡社（今台中縣神岡鄉）原住民開墾貓霧捒。
一七一九年	康熙五十八年	◎施世榜開拓東螺堡、八堡圳。

Taiwan Timeline: The Cing Era

Year (Western / Imperial calendars)		Major events in Taiwan
1684	The 23rd year of the Kangsi reign of Cing Emperor Shengzu	◎Taiwan Prefecture School, Taiwan County School and Fongshan County School are established.
1686	Kangsi Year 25	◎Hakkas settle Sia-Danshuei Plains (present-day Pingdong).
1694	Kangsi Year 35	◎Prefct Gao Gongcian edits "Taiwan Prefecture Gazette."
1697	Kangsi Year 36	◎Yu Yonghe mines sulfur in the North, recording his experiences in his "Yu Yonghe's tale of Formosa: a History of Seventeenth Century Taiwan" the following year.
1699	Kangsi Year 38	◎The plains indigenous people in Tunsiao Village rebel against abuse by Chinese interpreters. Tribes in Danshuei and Beitou villages join in rebellion.
1709	Kangsi Year 48	◎Chen Laijhang settle Dajiala (present-day Siyuan in Taipei).
1711	Kangsi Year 50	◎Cing Government decrees that mainlanders settling in Taiwan must register such with authorities in their hometown and return to that location within a prescribed period of time.
1714	Kangsi Year 53	◎Cing Government decrees that residents who wish to travel north of Dajiah River must obtain a permit from the government. Danshuei in the north is considered "beyond the realm of civilization."
1716	Kangsi Year 55	◎Indigenous people in Anli (present-day Shengang Township, Taichung County) settle Maowushu (Babuza).
1719	Kangsi Year 58	◎Shih Shihbang builds Dongluo Township and Babao Canal.

年代		台灣大事記
一七二〇年	康熙五十九年	◎泉州人施長齡、吳洛，客家人張振萬等拓墾台北平原。
一七二一年	康熙六十年	◎朱一貴、杜君英反清，失敗被斬。 ◎阿里山、水沙連各社反抗通事（至一七二二年）。
一七二二年	康熙六十一年	◎南路閩粵械鬥。一七二三年又起。
一七二三年	清世宗雍正元年	◎清朝政府設置彰化縣，及淡水、澎湖廳。 ◎藍鼎元著《平台紀略》。
一七二四年	雍正二年	◎淡水拳山莊居民開拓霧里薛圳（景美、新店一帶）。
一七二七年	雍正五年	◎清朝政府不准攜眷過台。 ◎黃叔璥著＜赤崁筆談＞、＜番俗六考＞。
一七三〇年	雍正八年	◎台灣人無妻室者逐回原籍。
一七三二年	雍正十年	◎清朝政府准許人民攜眷來台。 ◎林武力聯沙轆、吞霄社圍彰化。
一七三四年	雍正十二年	◎嚴防人民渡台。
一七三八年	清高宗乾隆三年	◎建艋舺龍山寺。
一七三九年	乾隆四年	◎禁止華人進入「番地」。

Year (Western / Imperial calendars)		Major events in Taiwan
1720	Kangsi Year 59	◎Two Cyuanjhou natives, Shih Changling and Wu Luo, along with Hakka Jhang Jhenwan, settle the Taipei Plain.
1721	Kangsi Year 60	◎Jhu I-gui and Du Jhun-ing lead a revolt against the Cing Government. Their rebellion fails and the pair are executed. ◎Indigenous people from Alishan and Shuishalien Villages rebel against abuse by interpreters. Rebellion lasts until 1722.
1722	Kangsi Year 61	◎Armed feuding break out between Hoklo and Hakka people in southern Taiwan. Violence erupts again in 1723.
1723	The 1st year of the Yongjheng reign of Cing Emperor Shihzong	◎Cing Government establishes Changhua County, Danshuei and Penghu sub-prefectures. Lan Dingyuan writes "A Brief History of Taiwan Pacification."
1724	Yongjheng Year 2	◎Cyuanshan villagers in Danshuei build Wulisyue irrigation canal (in present-day Jingmei/Sindian vicinity).
1727	Yongjheng Year 5	◎Cing Government prohibits bringing families to Taiwan. Huang Shujing writes "Notes on Chihkan" and "Six Inquiries Into the Customs of the Savages."
1730	Yongjheng Year 8	◎Settlers without families on Taiwan are ordered to return to the mainland.
1732	Yongjheng Year 10	◎Cing Government authorizes bringing families to Taiwan. Lin Wuli organizes tribes in Shalu and Tunsiao Villages laying siege to Jhanghua County.
1734	Yongjheng Year 12	◎Travel to Taiwan is strictly prohibited.
1738	The 3rd year of the Cianlong reign of Cing Emperor Gaozong	◎Longshan Temple is erected in Mengjia (present-day Wanhua District, Taipei City).
1739	Cianlong Year 4	◎Chinese settlers are prohibited from entering "savage lands."

年代		台灣大事記
一七四四年	乾隆九年	◎噍吧哖四社平埔族遷至荖濃溪與楠梓仙溪。
一七四五年	乾隆十年	◎泉州人沈用至錫口（今台北松山）拓墾，閩南人到桃澗堡開墾。
一七四七年	乾隆十二年	◎客家人至貓裡（即苗栗）。
一七五五年	乾隆二十年	◎淡水擺接堡墾戶林成祖開闢大安圳（從中和到板橋至土城）。
一七五九年	乾隆二十四年	◎規定華人買番地，必須納「番租」。
一七六八年	乾隆三十三年	◎黃教攻擊岡山營房，焚大目降（今台南縣新化）汛房，攻斗六門。
一七八一年	乾隆四十六年	◎閩南人與平埔族秀朗社（今台北縣永和一帶）訂約開墾深坑埔。
一七八二年	乾隆四十七年	◎彰化因賭博爭執，引起大規模漳泉械鬥，水師為鎮壓亂事殺了兩百多人。
一七八六年	乾隆五十一年	◎鹿港龍山寺落成。

Year (Western / Imperial calendars)		Major events in Taiwan
1744	Cianlong Year 9	◎Plains indigenous people from four villages in Jiaobanian move to the area between the Laonong and Nanzihsian Rivers.
1745	Cianlong Year 10	◎Cyuanjhou native Shen Yong settle Sikou (present-day Songshan District, Taipei City). Hoklo residents of Fengshan move north to Taojian Township (near present-day Taoyuan County) to farm.
1747	Cianlong Year 12	◎Hakka settlers move into Maoli (present-day Miaoli).
1755	Cianlong Year 20	◎Ling Chengzu, a settler at Baijie Township in Danshuei, begins excavation of Da-An Irrigation Canal system (irrigating an area encompassing present-day Jhonghe, Banciao and Tucheng in Taipei County).
1759	Cianlong Year 24	◎Special tax levied against Chinese purchasing "savage lands."
1768	Cianlong Year 33	◎Huang Jiao attacks Cing garrison at Gangshan, burning the Damujiang Barracks (present-day Sinhua, Tainan County), and launches assault on Doulioumen.
1781	Cianlong Year 46	◎Hoklo and plains indigenous people from Sioulang Village (present-day Yonghe, Taipei County) make agreement to settle Shenkeng.
1782	Cianlong Year 47	◎A dispute over gambling interests leads to large-scale armed conflict between Cyuanjhou and Jhangjhou people in Changhua. In suppressing the chaos, the Cing naval commander executes 200 people.
1786	Cianlong Year 51	◎Lugang's Lungshan Temple is built.

年代		台灣大事記
一七八七年	乾隆五十二年	◎林爽文之亂。 ◎禁止人民攜眷來台。
一七八八年	乾隆五十三年	◎實施屯番制。
一七九五年	乾隆六十年	◎吳沙占墾頭圍（宜蘭頭城）。 ◎陳周全反清。
一七九六年	清仁宗嘉慶三年	◎王士俊在竹塹開設私塾，鄭用錫等人入學就讀。
一七九七年	嘉慶四年	◎蛤仔蘭（宜蘭）因爭奪墾地引起泉籍、粵籍分類械鬥。
一八〇四年	嘉慶九年	◎彰化平埔族在潘賢文率領之下，遷徙至蛤仔蘭。
一八〇五年	嘉慶十年	◎海盜蔡牽攻擊淡水與鹿耳門等地，並劫走商船。
一八〇九年	嘉慶十四年	◎淡水漳籍、泉籍之間的糾紛事件，引發分類械鬥並蔓延至彰化、嘉義。 ◎大龍峒保安宮落成。
一八一四年	嘉慶十九年	◎隘首黃林旺、陳大用、郭百年侵入水裡、埔里，至一八一七年官府 將華人佃戶逐出埔里社，立碑禁止進入。
一八一七年	嘉慶二十二年	◎淡水廳在竹塹設立儒學。

Year (Western / Imperial calendars)		Major events in Taiwan
1787	Cianlong Year 52	◎Lin Shuangwun leads failed attempt to take over Taiwan. ◎Cing Government prohibits people from bringing families to Taiwan.
1788	Cianlong Year 53	◎Cing implements military colony system in Taiwan.
1795	Cianlong Year 60	◎Touwei (present-day Toucheng area in Yilan County) opened to cultivation. ◎Chen Jhoucyuan rebels against the Ning.
1796	The 3rd year of Jiacing reign of Cing Emperor Renzong	◎Wang Shihjyun opens private school in Jhucian. Jheng Yongsi and others go on to study there.
1797	Jiacing Year 4	◎In Kavalan (present-day Yilan County), land rights disputes lead to armed conflict between area Hakka and Cyuanjhou people.
1804	Jiacing Year 9	◎Led by Pan Sianwen, the Plains indigenous people from the Jhanghua region move north to Kavalan.
1805	Jiacing Year 10	◎The pirate Cai Cian attacks Danshuei, Luermen and other areas, seizing merchant vessels.
1809	Jiacing Year 14	◎Ethnic tension between Jhangjhou and Cyuanjhou peoples escalates into armed conflict that spreads to Jhanghua and Chiayi. ◎The Baoan Temple in Dalongdong is built.
1814	Jiacing Year 19	◎Guard-post leaders Huang Linwang, Chen Dayong and Guo Bainian occupy the indigenous villages of Shuili and Puli until 1817, when government troops drive Chinese tenant farmers out of Puli and post "No Entry" signs.
1817	Jiacing Year 22	◎Danshuei Sub-Prefecture Government sets up Confucian School in Jhucian (present-day Hsinchu).

年代		台灣大事記
一八二三年	清宣宗道光三年	◎噶瑪蘭軍工匠林詠春反清，攻青潭、大坪林。
一八二五年	道光五年	◎東勢角、葫蘆墩平埔族七百人遷移至埔里社。
一八三一年	道光十一年	◎客家人姜秀鑾、閩南人周邦正與官府合資設「金廣福」墾號，開拓北埔（在今新竹縣）。
一八三八年	道光十八年	◎英國人至淡水以鴉片換樟腦。
一八四一年	道光二十一年	◎英國納爾不達號（Nerbudda）在基隆觸礁，四百多人被俘、被殺。
一八五三年	清文宗咸豐三年	◎淡水發生漳泉械鬥，同安人敗退至大稻埕。
一八五八年	咸豐八年	◎天津條約簽訂，台灣開港。
一八五九年	咸豐九年	◎北部多處（淡水港仔嘴、加蚋仔、枋橋、芝蘭莊、桃仔園）發生漳泉械鬥，延續至一八六〇年。
一八六〇年	咸豐十年	◎北京條約簽訂，開放淡水、安平港。
一八六二年	清穆宗同治元年	◎戴潮春反清。
一八六五年	同治四年	◎一八六四年戴潮春被捕，一八六五年嚴辦戰死，戴軍始衰。
一八六七年	同治六年	◎美籍船羅發號（Rover）事件。

Year (Western / Imperial calendars)		Major events in Taiwan
1823	The 3rd year of the Daoguang reign of Cing Emperor Syuanzong	◎Lin Yongchun, a Kevalan tribal armorer, rebels against the Cing Government, attacking Cingtan and Dapinglin.
1825	Daoguang Year 5	◎Around 700 plains indigenous people from Dongshihjiao and Huludun move to Puli.
1831	Daoguang Year 11	◎Jiang Siouluan, a Hakka, and Jhou Bangjheng, a Hoklo, jointly found the Jinguangfu Corporation with government assistance and begin cultivating fields around Beipu (present-day Hsinchu County).
1838	Daoguang Year 18	◎The British enter Danshuei to trade opium for camphor.
1841	Daoguang Year 21	◎An English vessel, the Nerbudda, hits a reef in Keelung Harbor. More than 400 people on board are killed or taken hostage.
1853	The 3rd year of the Sianfeng reign of Cing Emperor Wenzong	◎In Danshuei the Jhangjhou and Cyuanjhou people engage in armed feduing. People from Tung-an retreat to Dadaocheng.
1858	Sianfeng Year 8	◎Treaty of Tianjin is signed; Taiwan is forced to open its ports.
1859	Sianfeng Year 9	◎Armed conflict between Jhangjhou and Cyanjhou settlers erupts in areas throughout the north (including present-day Jiangzicui, Shuangyuan, Banciao, Shihlin and Taoyuan). The violence continues into 1860.
1860	Sianfeng Year 10	◎Convention of Peking is signed; Danshuei and Anping ports opened.
1862	The first year of the Tongjhih reign of Cing Emperor Muzong	◎Dai Chaochun rebels against the Cing.
1865	Tongjhih Year 4	◎1864 Dai Chaochun is captured. Yan Ban is killed in battle the following year and Dai's forces begin to decline.
1867	Tongjhih Year 6	◎The Rover (an American vessel) Incident occurs.

年代		台灣大事記
一八七三年	同治十二年	◎牡丹社事件（至一八七四年結束）。
一八七四年	同治十三年	◎沈葆禎奉命辦理台灣等處海防。
一八七五年	清德宗光緒元年	◎設置台北府，管轄淡水、新竹、宜蘭三縣，並設基隆、卑南、埔里社三廳。
一八七六年	光緒二年	◎英人開八斗子煤礦。 ◎一八七六至一八七八年鎮壓東部原住民。
一八七七年	光緒三年	◎架設台南到旗後的電報線。
一八七八年	光緒四年	◎獎勵拓墾「番地」。
一八七九年	光緒五年	◎滬尾馬偕醫館成立。
一八八二年	光緒八年	◎馬偕創設牛津學堂，成為台灣北部第一間教授西學的學校。
一八八三年	光緒九年	◎中法越南戰爭。一八八四年起法軍封鎖北部台灣，並占領澎湖。
一八八五年	光緒十一年	◎台灣建省。
一八八六年	光緒十二年	◎設南北兩府清賦總局，在台北設置電報局、茶厘、稅厘、礦務總局。
一八八七年	光緒十三年	◎清朝政府籌辦台灣鐵路，並連接台灣與福州（福建）的海底電報線。
一八八八年	光緒十四年	◎設郵政總局；實施由小租戶直接納稅。

Year (Western / Imperial calendars)		Major events in Taiwan
1873	Tongjhih Year 12	◎The Mudan Village Incident occurs (not resolved until 1874).
1874	Tongjhih Year 13	◎Shen Baojhen sets up sea defenses for Taiwan.
1875	The first year of the Guangsyu reign of Cing Emperor Dezong	◎Taipei Prefecture is established, with jurisdiction over Danshuei, Hsinchu, and Yilan Counties as well as the Keelung, primaba, and Puli Village Sub prefectures.
1876	Guangsyu Year 2	◎The British begin mining coal in Badouzih. ◎1876-1878 Government launches suppression campaigns against indigenous peoples in several eastern areas.
1877	Guangsyu Year 3	◎Telegraph cables are laid from Tainan to Cihou.
1878	Guangsyu Year 4	◎Cing Government encourages settlers to settle "savage land."
1879	Guangsyu Year 5	◎Canadian Missionary George Leslie Mackay founds Mackay Hospital in Huwei (present-day Danshuei).
1882	Guangsyu Year 8	◎Mackay founds Oxford College, the first school of Western studies in northern Taiwan.
1883	Guangsyu Year 9	◎Sino-French War erupts in Vietnam. In 1884 the French blockade northern Taiwan and occupy Penghu.
1885	Guangsyu Year 11	◎Taiwan Province is established.
1886	Guangsyu Year 12	◎Tax bureaus are set up in the north and south. The Telegraph Bureau, Tea Bureau, Tax Bureau and Bureau of Mines are set up in Taipei.
1887	Guangsyu Year 13	◎The government begins to build railways. Undersea telegraph cables are laid between Taiwan and Fujhou, Fujian Province.
1888	Guangsyu Year 14	◎Postal system is established. Small-rent direct tax remittance system is implemented.

年代		台灣大事記
一八九五年	光緒二十一年 日本明治二十八年	◎四月十七日：馬關條約中承認朝鮮國獨立，大清帝國割讓台灣、遼東給日本。 ◎五月二十五日：唐景崧、丘逢甲等人成立「台灣民主國」。 ◎五月二十九日：日軍登陸澳底鹽寮（位於現今的台北縣貢寮鄉）。 ◎六月四日：唐景崧內渡回中國。台灣人持續抵抗日軍長達五個月。 ◎十月十九日：劉永福逃離台灣，「台灣民主國」亡。
一八九六年	明治二十九年	◎三月三十日：日本政府公布「六三法」。
一八九九年	明治三十二年	◎日本殖民政府依「匪徒刑罰令」，處死一〇二三人。 ◎開始修築從基隆到高雄的縱貫鐵路。 ◎台灣銀行開始營業。 ◎台北師範開校。 ◎台北自來水、排水溝系統完成。
一九〇〇年	明治三十三年	◎台北、台南開始設立公用電話。
一九〇一年	明治三十四年	◎台灣總督府公布「總督府專賣局官制」，樟腦、鴉片、食鹽為專賣品，並設於同一局內。
一九〇三年	明治三十六年	◎第一個水力發電所在桃園龜山成立。 ◎成立「臨時台灣番地調查事務委員會」。

Year (Western / Imperial calendars)		Major events in Taiwan
1895	Guangsyu Year 21 Meiji year 28 of Japan	◎17 April: Through the Treaty of Maguan (Treaty of Shimonoseki in Japanese) the Chinese (Cing) Government recognizes Korea as an independent nation and cedes Taiwan and the Liaodong Peninsula to Japan. ◎25 May: Tang Jingsong and Ciou Fongjia establish the Taiwan Republic. ◎29 May: Japanese forces land in Taiwan at Yanliao in Aodi area (near present-day Gongliao Township in Taipei County). ◎4 June: Tang Jingsong flees to China; Taiwanese continue resistance against Japan for another five months. ◎19 October: Liou Yongfu flees Taiwan; the Taiwan Republic collapses.
1896	Meiji year 29	◎30 March: The Japanese Government promulgates "The 63rd Law."
1899	Meiji year 32	◎The Japanese colonial government executes 1,023 people in accordance with the "Statute for the Punishment of Bandits." ◎Construction begins on the North-South Railroad from Keelung to Kaohsiung. ◎The Bank of Taiwan opens. ◎The Taipei Normal (Teachers') College is established. ◎Taipei tap water and sewerage systems completed.
1900	Meiji year 33	◎Public telephones set up in Taipei and Tainan.
1901	Meiji year 34	◎The Taiwan Governor-General's Office promulgates the "Colonial Monopoly System" monopolizing trade in camphor, opium and salt and consolidating the trade under one bureau.
1903	Meiji year 36	◎The first hydroelectric power station is established at Gueishan, Taoyuan. ◎The "Taiwan Provisional Savages' Land Investigative Commission" is established.

年代		台灣大事記
一九〇五年	明治三十八年	◎十月一日：第一次戶口普查。
一九〇六年	明治三十九年	◎統一度量衡。
一九〇七年	明治四十年	◎四月二十七日：「北埔事件」爆發。
一九〇八年	明治四十一年	◎二月二十九日：公布「官設埤圳規則」。 ◎四月二十日：縱貫鐵路全線通車。 ◎高雄港正式開工築港（一九〇八年至一九一二年）。
一九〇九年	明治四十二年	◎埔里社支廳泰雅族二十六社反抗。
一九一〇年	明治四十三年	◎五年理番計畫開始。
一九一一年	明治四十四年	◎統一台灣貨幣。 ◎阿里山鐵路全線通車。 ◎十月二十六日：任用本地人為巡查（基層警員）。
一九一四年	大正三年	◎第一次世界大戰爆發（一九一四年至一九一八年）。 ◎鎮壓太魯閣原住民。
一九一五年	大正四年	◎余清芳以神明指示為由，號召西來庵信徒反抗日軍，日軍屠殺近千人。 ◎台灣總督府開發八仙山、宜蘭太平山森林。
一九一九年	大正八年	◎台北市公共汽車開始營業。

Year (Western / Imperial calendars)		Major events in Taiwan
1905	Meiji year 38	◎1 October: Taiwan's first residents population census is taken.
1906	Meiji year 39	◎Weights and measures are standardized.
1907	Meiji year 40	◎27 April: "Beipu Incident" and Japanese suppression.
1908	Meiji year 41	◎29 February: Regulations Governing Government Irrigation Works promulgated. ◎20 April: Completion of the North-South Railway. ◎Construction of Kaohsiung Harbor formally begins (1908-1912).
1909	Meiji year 42	◎26 Villages of the Atayal people near Puli Village Subprefecture rise up to resist the Japanese.
1910	Meiji year 43	◎Five-year plan for eradicating or assimilating the "savages" begins.
1911	Meiji year 44	◎Taiwan's currency unified. ◎Alishan railway completed. ◎26 October: Taiwanese are given positions as patrol officials (lowest-level police officers).
1914	Taisho year 3	◎World War I breaks out (1914-1918). ◎Extensive annihilation campaign against the Truku people begins in the area around present-day Taroko National Park.
1915	Taisho year 4	◎Yu Cingfang leads his followers in uprising known as the Silai Temple Incident; Japanese troops massacre about 1,000. ◎Taiwan Governor-General's Office begins exploitation of ancient forests around Basian Mountain and Taiping Mountain in nowadays Yilan County.
1919	Taisho year 8	◎Public buses begin operation in Taipei City.

年代		台灣大事記
一九二一年	大正十年	◎一月十七日：「台灣文化協會」成立。 ◎「台灣議會設置請願運動」開始。
一九二三年	大正十二年	◎黃呈聰發表〈論普及白話文的新使命〉，黃朝琴發表〈漢文改革論〉，蔡培火發表〈台灣新文學運動與羅馬字〉。首創台灣白話文運動先河。
一九二四年	大正十三年	◎七星畫壇成立（倪蔣懷、陳澄波、陳英聲、陳承藩、藍蔭鼎、陳植棋、陳銀用）。
一九二五年	大正十四年	◎十月二十二日：爆發「二林事件」，蔗農為爭取權益與警察發生衝突。
一九二六年	昭和元年	◎三月二十七日：台東到花蓮鐵路線開通。 ◎六月二十八日：「台灣農民組合」成立。
一九二九年	昭和四年	◎糾紛二十多年的「竹林事件」，被迫解決；日本殖民政府要求各庄出錢購回竹林，繼續抗爭的農民則以警力鎮壓。
一九三〇年	昭和五年	◎四月十日：嘉南大圳通水起用。 ◎九月二十二日：農民包圍學甲、下營、佳里、麻豆各地庄役所，要求減免水租。 ◎十月二十七日：發生「霧社事件」。
一九三四年	昭和九年	◎五月十一日：日本四大財閥決定合辦台鋁公司。

Year (Western / Imperial calendars)		Major events in Taiwan
1921	Taisho year 10	◎17 January: The Taiwan Culture Association is established. ◎Petitions for the establishment of a Taiwan Representative Assembly begin.
1923	Taisho year 12	◎Huang Chengcong publishes "The New Mission for the Vernacular Language." Huang Chaocin publishes "The Revolution in Chinese Language." Cai Peihuo publishes "The Roman Alphabet and the New Taiwanese Literary Movement." The vernacular writing movement in Taiwan begins.
1924	Taisho year 13	◎The "Seven Stars" Art Forum is established (comprised of Ni Jianghuai, Chen Chengpo, Chen Yingsheng, Chen Chengfan, Lan Yinding, Chen Jhihci and Chen Yinyong).
1925	Taisho year 14	◎22 October: Erlin Incident occurs when sugarcane farmers clash with police over rights.
1926	Showa year 1	◎27 March: Taitung-Hualien railroad opens. ◎28 June: Taiwan Farmers Association is established.
1929	Showa year 4	◎The Bamboo Forest Incident, a dispute that had been ongoing for more than 20 years, finally ends. The Japanese colonial government requires all the villagers concerned to buy back the Bamboo Forest. Dissatisfied farmers continue opposition and are suppressed by police.
1930	Showa year 5	◎10 April: Jianan Irrigation Canal begins operation. ◎22 September: Farmers surround township offices in Syuejia, Siaying, Jiali, Madou and other areas demanding a reduction in water rates. ◎27 October: Wushe Uprising of the Atayal People.
1934	Showa year 9	◎11 May: Japan's four major financial groups agree to jointly invest in the Taiwan Aluminum Corporation.

年代		台灣大事記
一九三五年	昭和十年	◎十一月二十二日：舉行台灣首次投票，選舉地方議員。
一九三六年	昭和十一年	◎三月三十日：松山機場竣工。
一九三七年	昭和十二年	◎六月一日：台灣船塢公司成立。 ◎七月七日：中日戰爭爆發，日本改派軍人為台灣總督。 ◎七月三十一日：日月潭第二期發電所竣工。
一九四〇年	昭和十五年	◎推行改用日本姓名運動。
一九四一年	昭和十六年	◎二月八日：台灣總督府公布禁止台灣人使用舊曆（陰曆）。 ◎四月十九日：「皇民奉公會」成立。 ◎十二月八日：日本轟炸美國的太平洋基地，開啟美日戰爭。
一九四二年	昭和十七年	◎日軍募集台灣人為「陸軍志願兵」。
一九四三年	昭和十八年	◎強迫農民交出白米，實施糧食管制與配給。 ◎強徵台、韓籍學生赴前線。
一九四五年	昭和二十年	◎美軍飛機轟炸台灣各地。 ◎八月十五日：日本無條件投降，也結束日本在台五十一年的統治。

Year (Western / Imperial calendars)		Major events in Taiwan
1935	Showa year 10	◎22 November: Taiwan's first elections are held for local assemblies.
1936	Showa year 11	◎30 March: Construction completed on Songshan Airport.
1937	Showa year 12	◎1 June: Taiwan Shipyard Corporation is established. ◎7 July: Sino-Japanese War breaks out. Japan appoints military Governor-General's of Taiwan. ◎31 July: The construction of the second phase of Sun Moon Lake power plant is completed.
1940	Showa year 15	◎Campaign begins promoting the use of Japanese family and given names for Taiwanese.
1941	Showa year 16	◎8 February: Taiwan Governor-General's Office announces prohibition of the use of lunar calendars. ◎19 April: Imperial Citizen Associations formed. ◎8 December: U.S. dedares war on Japan following Japanese attack on Pearl Harbor.
1942	Showa year 17	◎Japanese recruit Taiwanese for "volunteer brigades."
1943	Showa year 18	◎Farmers are forced to hand over rice harvests. Food rationing is implemented. ◎Taiwanese and Korean students are forced to join the military at the front.
1945	Showa year 20	◎American air force bombs Taiwan. ◎15 August: Japan surrenders unconditionally and 51 years of Japanese rule in Taiwan comes to an end.

年代		台灣大事記
一九四五年	民國三十四年	◎ 八月十五日：日本天皇宣布接受「波茨坦宣言」，無條件投降。 ◎ 十至十一月：國民黨政府軍隊與陳儀來台接收。 ◎ 十二月：米價暴漲，各地物價漲為戰爭結束時的十倍。
一九四七年	民國三十六年	◎二二八事件。
一九四八年	民國三十七年	◎「國語推行委員會」成立，後來演變成在學校講台語的學生要罰錢，並在胸前掛牌警告。
一九四九年	民國三十八年	◎ 五月：實施戒嚴。 ◎ 十二月：國民黨政府遷移到台灣。 ◎ 土地改革開始，推行「三七五減租」。 ◎ 台灣發生惡性通貨膨脹。 ◎ 實行「貨幣改革」，發行新台幣，舊台幣四萬元換新台幣一元。
一九五〇年	民國三十九年	◎ 蔣介石在台「復行視事」，陳誠任行政院院長。 ◎ 發行愛國獎券（至一九八八年停止）。 ◎ 韓戰爆發，美國第七艦隊進入台灣海峽，宣布台灣海峽中立化，解除台灣受中共攻擊的危機。 ◎ 蔣介石提出「一年準備，兩年反攻，三年掃蕩，五年成功」的口號。
一九五一年	民國四十年	◎ 美國經濟援助正式進入台灣（至一九六五年）。
一九五二年	民國四十一年	◎ 髮禁開始，中學男生頭髮不得超過三公分，女生短髮長度不過耳際。 ◎「中國青年反共救國團」正式成立，主任為蔣經國。

Taiwan Timeline: The Post-World War II Era

Year (Western / Minguo)		Major events in Taiwan
1945	**Minguo year 34**	◎August 15: The Japanese emperor accepts the Potsdam Declaration and offers unconditional surrender. ◎October/November: The KMT Army and Chen Yi arrive in Taiwan. ◎December: The price of rice skyrockets and the price of goods increases by as much as ten times compared to levels just at the end of WWⅡ.
1947	**Minguo year 36**	◎The Feburary 28 Incident.
1948	**Minguo year 37**	◎The "Mandarin Promotion Commission" is established and its policies are eventually twisted so that students who speak Taiwanese in school are punished.
1949	**Minguo year 38**	◎May: Martial law is imposed. ◎December: The KMT Government formally relocates to Taiwan. ◎The land reform begins with the "37.5%" rent reduction. ◎Taiwan's inflation rate soars. ◎"Monatary reform": Old Taiwan Dollars are replaced by New Taiwan Dollars (NT) at a rate of 40,000 to 1.
1950	**Minguo year 39**	◎Chiang Kai-shek resumes office as the President. Chen Cheng is named Premier. ◎Patriotism Lottery begins (continues through 1988). ◎The Korean War breaks out and the U.S. 7th Fleet enters the Taiwan Strait to prevent a communist attack on Taiwan. ◎Chiang Kai-Shek first uses the slogan: "Year 1 – Prepare; Year 2 – Attack; Year 3 – Sweep the Enemy; Year 5– Success".
1951	**Minguo year 40**	◎U.S. aid program officially begins (continues through 1965).
1952	**Minguo year 41**	◎Hairstyle restrictions are implemented in middle schools (boys' hair could not exceed 3 cm in length, and girls' hair could not extend beyond their ears). ◎The China Youth Corps is organized with Chiang Ching-kuo serving as Director.

年代		台灣大事記
一九五三年	民國四十二年	◎ 四年經濟建設計畫，實施「耕者有其田」政策。 ◎ 各中等學校實施軍訓。
一九五四年	民國四十三年	◎ 簽署「中美共同防禦條約」。 ◎ 滯留韓國一萬四千二百零九名「反共義士」來台。
一九五八年	民國四十七年	◎ 八二三炮戰（第二次台海危機）。此後二十年中共單日炮擊金門，雙日停火（單打雙不打）。
一九五九年	民國四十八年	◎ 熱帶性低氣壓引發八七水災，三十萬名民眾無家可歸。 ◎ 台灣人口密度世界最高，蔣夢麟呼籲節育未被接受。
一九六〇年	民國四十九年	◎ 當局以涉嫌叛亂罪名，逮捕《自由中國》雜誌編輯雷震。 ◎ 中橫公路全線通車。 ◎ 國民大會通過「動員戡亂時期臨時條款」修正案，總統連任不受兩任限制。
一九六二年	民國五十一年	◎ 第一家電視台「台視」開播。 ◎ 台灣警備總部通令全國，自六月一日起查禁「三年」等流行歌曲。
一九六三年	民國五十二年	◎ 農業普查結果，台灣一千多萬人口中半數從事農業。 ◎ 紀政創下女子百米短跑世界紀錄。
一九六四年	民國五十三年	◎ 彭明敏、謝聰敏、魏廷朝等人因為「台灣人民自救宣言」被逮捕。 ◎ 嘉南地區發生大地震，災情慘重。

Year (Western / Minguo)		Major events in Taiwan
1953	Minguo year 42	◎The Four Year Economic Plan begins. The "Land-to-the-Tiller" program is implemented. ◎All middle schools begin military training.
1954	Minguo year 43	◎Mutual Defense Treaty signed with the United States. ◎14,209 "anti-communist patriots" stranded in Korea are brought to Taiwan.
1958	Minguo year 47	◎The "August 23 attack" sets off the second major crisis in the Taiwan Strait. For twenty years China shells Kinmen every other day.
1959	Minguo year 48	◎Three hundred thousand people left homeless from flooding on August 7th. ◎Population density in Taiwan becomes the highest in the world. Authorities reject recommendation from Jiang Menglin to curb population growth.
1960	Minguo year 49	◎Authorities arrest Lei Chen, editor of "Free China" on charges of sedition. ◎The first Central Cross-island road is completed. ◎The National Assembly adopts an amendment to the "Articles of National Mobilization for the Suppression of the Communist Rebellion" witch stipulates that the president may be re-elected without being subject to the two-term restriction.
1962	Minguo year 51	◎Taiwan's first television station TTV（Taiwan Television）begins broadcasting. ◎The Taiwan Garrison Command bans "Three Years" and other popular songs.
1963	Minguo year 52	◎A survey shows more than half of Taiwan's population (some ten million) is engaged in agriculture. ◎Chi Cheng breaks the world record for the women's 100-meter sprint.
1964	Minguo year 53	◎Prof. Peng Mingmin, Sie Congmin, Wei Tingchao and several others are arrested for their "Taiwan Self Preservation Declaration." ◎Major damage results from an earthquake in the Chiayi and Tainan area.

年代		台灣大事記
一九六五年	民國五十四年	◎ 美國大規模介入越戰，台灣成為駐越南美軍的補給基地及渡假中心，酒吧等供美軍娛樂的行業大量興起，並留下二、三千名的「美亞兒童」。
一九六六年	民國五十五年	◎ 美式文化入侵，西洋舞蹈、音樂、服裝、髮型等大受歡迎。 ◎ 為「端正社會風氣」，警察負起整頓年輕人儀容的工作。 ◎ 高雄加工出口區落成。
一九六七年	民國五十六年	◎ 總統明令公布設置「動員戡亂時期國家安全會議」，為之前的「國防會議」合法化。
一九六八年	民國五十七年	◎ 義務教育延長為九年。 ◎ 行政院公布台灣地區家庭計畫辦法，實施節育。 ◎ 為求建築物安全無虞，三樓以上樓房一律改用鋼筋混凝土結構。
一九六九年	民國五十八年	◎ 電視安裝率大增。 ◎ 金龍少棒隊獲得世界冠軍，促成台灣全民棒球運動。
一九七〇年	民國五十九年	◎ 台灣赴釣魚台作業漁船四百艘遭日本巡邏艇干擾。 ◎ 肺結核病患者共四萬六千人，二萬人治療中。
一九七一年	民國六十年	◎ 美國擬將釣魚台交予日本，政府不願得罪美、日而低調處理，學生發起保釣運動。 ◎ 我國宣布退出聯合國。聯合國大會決議由「中華人民共和國」繼承「中華民國」在聯合國的席位。 ◎ 蔣介石於第三次國家安全會議提出「莊敬自強，處變不驚」的呼籲，成為面對外交困境時最常用的精神標語。 ◎ 台灣出國、移民人數增加。

Year (Western / Minguo)		Major events in Taiwan
1965	Minguo year 54	◎Vietnam conflict escalates. Taiwan becomes a major supply station and relaxation destination for U.S. military; bars and the sex service industry increases, producing two to three thousand "Amerasian babies" in Taiwan.
1966	Minguo year 55	◎American popular culture hits Taiwan creating a craze for American dance, music, fashion and hairstyles. ◎In order to ensure a proper "social morality," Taiwan police are given responsibility for cracking down on the "improper appearance" of the youth. ◎First Export Processing Zone opens in Kaohsiung.
1967	Minguo year 56	◎The "National Security Council During the Period of National Mobilization for the Suppression of the Communist Rebellion" is established.
1968	Minguo year 57	◎Compulsory education is extended from six years to nine years. ◎The Executive Yuan announces a national birth control policy. ◎In order to ensure security of buildings, all structures of three floors or more are required to use reinforced concrete.
1969	Minguo year 58	◎Number of households with televisions increases dramatically. ◎Golden Dragon team from Taiwan wins the Little League World Series, setting off a nation-wide baseball craze.
1970	Minguo year 59	◎Four hundred Taiwanese fishing vessels encounter harassment from a Japanese patrol boat in the Diaoyutai Islands. ◎Over 46,000 people are afflicted with tuberculosis, 20,000 undergoing treatment.
1971	Minguo year 60	◎The U.S. plans to "return" the Diaoyutai Islands to Japan. A student movement erupts following the government's inaction to this event for fear of upsetting the U.S. and Japan. ◎Taiwan withdraws from the United Nations prior to the vote on whether the People's Republic of China would take over the seat of the Republic of China (Taiwan). ◎Chiang Kai-shek coins the slogan "stay firm in the face of adversity" to meet Taiwan's rapidly declining international status. ◎Substantial increases of people going abroad and emigrating from Taiwan.

年代		台灣大事記
一九七二年	民國六十一年	◎ 日本與我斷交，各地發起抵制日貨運動。 ◎ 台灣人口超過一千五百萬人。
一九七三年	民國六十二年	◎ 第一次石油危機。 ◎ 蔣經國正式提出九大建設，隔年又增加核能發電廠一項。
一九七四年	民國六十三年	◎ 石油危機導致台灣物價上漲兩倍。 ◎ 省主席謝東閔推動「客廳即工廠」，免徵營利事業所得稅，全台數萬家庭參與。 ◎ 我國少棒、青少棒、青棒分別獲得世界賽冠軍。
一九七五年	民國六十四年	◎ 蔣介石去世，蔣經國出任中國國民黨黨主席。
一九七六年	民國六十五年	◎ 教育部公布國中小校長包庇老師惡補者一律免職。 ◎ 今年是龍年，出現嬰兒潮，有四十三萬餘嬰兒出生。 ◎ 公布「廣播電視法」，規定廣播播音以國語為主，方言應逐年減少。
一九七七年	民國六十六年	◎ 鄉土文學論戰。 ◎ 教育部禁止教師在補習班兼課、學生在補習班補習。 ◎ 因桃園縣長選舉舞弊引發「中壢事件」。
一九七八年	民國六十七年	◎ 蔣經國出任第六任總統。 ◎ 美國宣布將與中華人民共和國建交，並將終止與我國外交關係及共同防禦條約。 ◎ 南北高速公路全線通車。

Year (Western / Minguo)		Major events in Taiwan
1972	Minguo year 61	◎Japan breaks diplomatic ties with Taiwan, resulting in boycotts of Japanese products throughout the island. ◎Taiwan's population breaks the 15 million mark.
1973	Minguo year 62	◎First world oil crisis. ◎Premier Chiang Ching-kuo announces the "Ten Major Constructions" plan, with the proposal for the Taiwan's first nuclear power plant following a year later.
1974	Minguo year 63	◎World oil prices result in a doubling of the price of consumer goods in Taiwan. ◎Taiwan Provincial Governor Hsieh Tong-min promotes "the living room is a factory" by exempting household factories from business income tax. Tens of thousands of households around the country participate. ◎Baseball teams representing Taiwan take first place at the Little League, Junior League and Senior League World Series.
1975	Minguo year 64	◎Chiang Kai-shek passes away. Chiang Ching-kuo takes over as head of the KMT.
1976	Minguo year 65	◎Ministry of Education announces the dismissal of all school principals that allow teachers to engage in exploitative tutoring practices. ◎The year of the Dragon: more than 430,000 children are born in this auspicious year. ◎The Broadcasting and Television Law stipulates that the majority of programs should be broadcast in Mandarin and that programs in other dialects should be gradually reduced.
1977	Minguo year 66	◎Country literature debate begins. ◎Rioting in Jhongli erupts after vote rigging was discovered in elections for the Taoyuan County magistrate. ◎Ministry of Education forbids teachers from teaching in cram schools and prohibits students from attending cram schools.
1978	Minguo year 67	◎Chiang Ching-kuo is elected as the President of the sixth term of the R.O.C. ◎U.S. announces it will establish diplomatic ties with the People's Republic of China and terminate diplomatic ties and the Mutual Defense Treaty with Taiwan. ◎The North-South Highway is opened to traffic.

年代		台灣大事記
一九七九年	民國六十八年	◎ 中（共）美宣布正式建交，美國與我斷交。 ◎ 美國總統卡特簽署「台灣關係法」。 ◎ 美麗島事件發生，警備總部逮捕美麗島政團人士，查封美麗島雜誌社。 ◎ 中正機場正式啟用。 ◎ 首座核能電廠完工。 ◎ 統一企業引進二十四小時營業連鎖便利商店，掀起流通業革命。
一九八○年	民國六十九年	◎ 新竹科學工業園區開幕。 ◎ 北迴鐵路正式通車。
一九八一年	民國七十年	◎ 美麗島事件後首次省市議員及縣市長選舉，國民黨獲得七十八％、黨外人士獲得二○％席次。 ◎ 鄧小平首倡一國兩制。
一九八二年	民國七十一年	◎ 台灣第一宗銀行搶案。 ◎ 中共飛行員吳榮根駕米格十九投奔自由，抵達韓國，此後「反共義士」、「投奔自由」事件不斷發生。
一九八三年	民國七十二年	◎ 行政院下令暫停進口廢五金、廢電線、電纜，但廢五金污染已經造成。
一九八四年	民國七十三年	◎ 美國速食連鎖店「麥當勞」登陸台灣。 ◎ 治安單位展開「一清專案」，黑道生態發生明顯變化。
一九八五年	民國七十四年	◎ 台北第十信用合作社爆發弊案，引發擠兌風潮。 ◎ 原住民要求恢復原有姓氏。 ◎ 屏東及鳳山兩市因垃圾傾倒問題產生糾紛。

Year (Western / Minguo)		Major events in Taiwan
1979	Minguo year 68	◎The U.S. establishes diplomatic relations with the PRC and severes relations with the R.O.C. ◎U.S. President Jimmy Carter signs the "Taiwan Relations Act." ◎Kaohsiung Incident: Taiwan Garrison Command arrests the editors of "Formosa Magazine" and sequesters the magazine's facilities. ◎C.K.S. Airport opens. ◎The first nuclear power plant is completed. ◎Uni-President Enterprises opens the first 24-hour convenience store ushering in a retail revolution in Taiwan.
1980	Minguo year 69	◎Hsinchu Science Park opens. ◎North Link Railroad is completed.
1981	Minguo year 70	◎First election after the Kaohsiung Incident: The KMT gets 78% of the seats in elections for county and city councils and magistrates. The remaining 20% go to "Dangwai"(outsiders of the KMT) . ◎Deng Siaoping introduces the concept of "one country, two systems."
1982	Minguo year 71	◎Taiwan's first bank robbery occurs. ◎Communist Chinese Pilot Wu Ronggen defects to South Korea in a MIG-19 jet starting what will become a wave of "freedom flights" by "Chinese anti-communist patriots."
1983	Minguo year 72	◎Executive Yuan announces a ban on imports of scrap metal, scrap cable and wire but the environmental effects are already widespread.
1984	Minguo year 73	◎The first MacDonald's opens in Taiwan setting off an onslaught from the world's fast food franchises. ◎Security officials begin a campaign against underground gangs.
1985	Minguo year 74	◎A corruption scandal erupts at the Tenth Credit Cooperative, causing a run on the bank. ◎Indigenous people demand the right to use their traditional surnames (instead of Chinese surnames). ◎A dispute arises between Pingtung and Fongshan townships over garbage disposal issues.

年代		台灣大事記
一九八六年	民國七十五年	◎ 鹿港「反杜邦」遊行，為民間環保抗議的開端。 ◎ 民主進步黨成立。
一九八七年	民國七十六年	◎ 解除戒嚴。 ◎ 開放大陸探親。
一九八八年	民國七十七年	◎ 解除報禁。 ◎ 蔣經國病逝，李登輝接任總統。 ◎ 「雅美青年聯誼會」在蘭嶼舉行反核示威遊行。 ◎ 中南部農民在台北請願遊行，演變成「五二〇」流血事件。 ◎ 原住民「還我土地」運動聯盟抗議。 ◎ 高雄林園居民抗議石化工業污染。
一九八九年	民國七十八年	◎ 中國發生震驚世界的「六四天安門事件」。
一九九〇年	民國七十九年	◎ 萬餘名學生靜坐、絕食抗議，要求解散國民大會，總統民選，並加速民主改革腳步。 ◎ 股市由一二四九五點暴跌至六三四六點。 ◎ 總統特赦美麗島事件政治犯。
一九九一年	民國八十年	◎ 宣布終止動員戡亂時期。
一九九二年	民國八十一年	◎ 政府公布二二八事件研究報告。 ◎ 南韓與我斷交。
一九九三年	民國八十二年	◎ 海基會董事長辜振甫與中國海協會會長汪道涵在新加坡舉行歷史性會談。 ◎ 中國飛機被劫持來台。 ◎ 有線電視法在立法院通過。 ◎ 新黨成立。

Year (Western / Minguo)		Major events in Taiwan
1986	Minguo year 75	◎An anti-Dupont march is held in the town of Lugang marking the beginning of civic environmental protests. ◎The Democratic Progressive Party is formed.
1987	Minguo year 76	◎Martial law ends after nearly forty years. ◎Residents of Taiwan are permitted to visit relatives in China.
1988	Minguo year 77	◎The ban on newspapers is lifted. ◎Chiang Ching-kuo passes away, Lee Teng-hui becomes President. ◎The Yami (Tao) Youth Group on Orchid Island hold a demonstration against the dumping of nuclear waste there. ◎A demonstration in Taipei by farmers from southern and central Taiwan turns bloody, resulting in what has become known as the "520 Incident." ◎The indigenous land rights movement begins to gain momentum. ◎Residents of the Linyuan Township in Kaohsiung launch protests against environmental pollution by the petrochemical industry.
1989	Minguo year 78	◎The bloody suppression of the Tiananmen pro-democracy protests shocks the world.
1990	Minguo year 79	◎Tens of thousands of students engage in sit-ins and hunger strikes to demand dissolution of the National Assembly, direct presidential elections and other democratic reforms. ◎Taiwan's stock market index slumps from 12495 to 6346. ◎Lee Teng-hui announces special amnesty for dissidents engaged in the Formosa Event.
1991	Minguo year 80	◎The "Period of National Mobilization for the Suppression of the Communist Rebellion" ends.
1992	Minguo year 81	◎The government publishes the "228 Incident White Paper." ◎South Korea severs diplomatic ties with Taiwan.
1993	Minguo year 82	◎Koo Chen-fu of the Straits Exchange Foundation and Wang Daohan of China's Association for Relations Across the Taiwan Strait hold historic talks in Singapore. ◎A Chinese passenger jet is hijacked and flown to Taiwan. ◎The Legislative Yuan passes the Cable Television Law. ◎The New Party is established.

年代		台灣大事記
一九九四年	民國八十三年	◎ 四一○教育改造萬人大遊行，以「推動教育現代化」為訴求。 ◎ 美國以台灣從事犀牛角與虎骨買賣為由，援引「培利修正案」，對台灣進行貿易制裁。 ◎ 五二九反核大遊行，將近三萬人參與。
一九九五年	民國八十四年	◎ 實施全民健保。 ◎ 李登輝總統訪問美國康乃爾大學，中國停止兩岸會談。 ◎ 中國在基隆外海一三○公里處進行東海五號海上演習。
一九九六年	民國八十五年	◎ 台灣第一次民選總統，中國宣布在基隆與高雄外海舉行第三次飛彈試射。美國派遣兩艘航空母艦來台灣海峽。 ◎ 李登輝、連戰當選台灣第一屆民選總統、副總統。 ◎ 台北縣林口鄉農會爆發鉅額超貸案，引發農會發生嚴重擠兌風潮。 ◎ 南非總統曼德拉宣布將於一九九七年底終止與我國邦交，並於隔年一月和中國建交。 ◎ 召開「國家發展會議」，會中達成數項憲政改革結論。其中「凍省」的決議，引發省政府、省議會的強烈反彈。
一九九七年	民國八十六年	◎ 總統召開高層治安會議，針對國內三大重大命案（劉邦友血案、彭婉如命案、白曉燕命案）至今未破造成社會不安，向國人致歉。民間社團發起五○四大遊行，對台灣的治安惡化向政府提出嚴重抗議。 ◎ 香港「回歸中國」受到全世界的注意，中國趁機宣傳一國兩制。 ◎ 縣市長選舉，民進黨當選過半。

Year (Western / Minguo)		Major events in Taiwan
1994	Minguo year 83	◎Tens of thousands take to the streets on April 10 to demand educational reforms. ◎United States imposes trade sanctions against Taiwan under the Pelly Amendment for their alleged trafficking in rhinoceros horn and tiger bones. ◎Over thirty thousand people march in anti-nuclear demonstration on 29 May.
1995	Minguo year 84	◎The National Health Insurance program begins. ◎Lee Teng-hui visits his alma mater Cornell University in the U.S.; China terminates all cross-strait talks. ◎China conducts war games 130 kilometers off the northeast coast of Taiwan.
1996	Minguo year 85	◎Taiwan holds it's first-ever direct presidential election. China announces a third round of missile testing to take place just off shore from Keelung in northern Taiwan and Kaohsiung in the south. The United States sends two aircraft carriers into the Taiwan Strait. ◎Lee Teng-hui and Lian Chan become the first directly elected President and Vice-President. ◎The Farmers Cooperative of Linkou is defrauded of over NT$400 million. The incident sets off a run on local banks and credit cooperatives around the nation. ◎South African President Nelson Mandela announces that diplomatic relations between his country and Taiwan will be severed at the end of 1997 followed by establishing relations with China in January 1998. ◎The National Development Conference results in a number of major resolutions concerning the Constitution, including perhaps the controversial decision to "freeze" the Taiwan Provincial Government. This decision receives fierce opposition from the Provincial Government and the Provincial Assembly.
1997	Minguo year 86	◎The President calls a high-level security meeting to denounce the failure of the government to solve three major murders (Actress Bai Bingbing's daughter, Taoyuan County Magistrate Liou Bangyou and women's rights activist Peng Wanru). The President apologizes to the nation but social groups organize massive demonstrations on May 4th to protest the decline of social order. ◎The world watches Hong Kong's "return to China" and China uses the opportunity to promote the "one country- two systems" ideology for addressing its relations with Taiwan. ◎The Democratic Progressive Party wins a majority of the year-end mayoral and county magistrate elections (with the exception of Taipei and Kaohsiung Cities).

年代		台灣大事記
一九九八年	民國八十七年	◎ 華航在大園鄉發生空難，機上乘客兩百六十多名乘客全部遇難，引發朝野對空中安全的嚴重關切。 ◎ 政府正式實施「隔週休二日制」，國人休閒生活明顯改變。 ◎ 行政院放寬財團法人買賣農地規定。 ◎ 美國總統柯林頓訪問上海、北京等地，發表對台「新三不」政策。 ◎ 北高市長及縣市議員、立法委員三合一選舉，國民黨當選過半。
一九九九年	民國八十八年	◎ 因應台灣加入世界貿易組織（WTO），酒類須依濃度提高價格以符合入世要求，因此爆發米酒囤積大戰。 ◎ 總統李登輝接受「德國之聲」訪問，首度提出台海兩岸為「特殊國與國」關係。 ◎ 教育部與大學聯招策進會宣布，自九十一年學年度起廢除爭議已久的聯考制度，改採多元入學的方案。 ◎ 發生芮氏規模七點三的九二一大地震，造成兩千多人死亡，八千多家房屋全倒。
二〇〇〇年	民國八十九年	◎ 民進黨總統候選人陳水扁贏得總統大選，結束長達五十多年的國民黨執政局面，完成首次政黨輪替。 ◎ 親民黨成立。 ◎ 國民大會三讀通過「國代虛級化」修憲案。 ◎ 台灣股市跌破五千點大關，打破「股市上萬點」的股票熱。 ◎ 行政院宣布停建核四（二〇〇一年決議續建）。
二〇〇五年	民國九十四年	◎ 新自然主義公司年度力作中英對照《台灣史10講》和《台灣歷史小百科》文字書，以及漫畫版《認識台灣歷史》（共10冊）出版。

Year (Western / Minguo)		Major events in Taiwan
1998	Minguo year 87	◎A China Airlines jet crashes in Taoyuan killing all 260 passengers, turning air safety into a major issue in Taiwan. ◎Government initiates alternating 5 and 6 day work-weeks, giving people more time for recreation. ◎The Executive Yuan lifts the ban on sales of agricultural land. ◎U.S. President Bill Clinton announces the "Three Nots" policy toward Taiwan during a visit to China. ◎The legislative, Taipei and Kaohsiung mayoral, and city/county council elections are held with the KMT retaining a majority.
1999	Minguo year 88	◎According to WTO regulations, wine taxes are to be raised. Rice wine hoarding results in a serious shortage. ◎Lee Teng-Hui raises the idea of "special state to state" relations across the Taiwan Strait during an interview with Deutsche Welle. ◎The Ministry of Education and the Joint College Entrance Committee decide that, effective 2002, the Multi-route Promotion Program for College-bound Seniors will be adopted to replace the entrance examination system. ◎Taiwan is hit by the deadliest earthquake in more than 60 years. The 7.3 magnitude quake claims more than 2,000 lives and more than 8,000 buildings collapse.
2000	Minguo year 89	◎Democratic Progress Party candidate Chen Shui-bian is elected president, ending the KMT's more than 50-year hold on the presidency in Taiwan. ◎The People First Party is established. ◎The National Assembly approves an amendment to reduce its powers and functions. ◎The Executive Yuan announces that the construction of the Forth Nuclear Power Plant will be halted. (In 2001, the Executive Yuan determines to resume construction of the Plant.)
2005	Minguo year 94	◎The bilingual "Ten Short Talks on Taiwan History" and "Mini-Encyclopedia of Taiwan History," and "A History of Taiwan in Comics" (10 voulume set) are published by Third Nature Publishing Company.

製作群介紹

◎總策劃、撰文（台灣史10講）
吳密察（Wu Mi-cha）
現職：台灣大學歷史系副教授
學歷：日本東京大學博士課程修了，專攻台灣史、
　　　日本近代史

◎英文策劃
文魯彬（Robin J. Winkler）
現職：台灣蠻野心足生態協會理事長、博仲法律事
　　　務所（本國與外國法事務律師事務所）合夥
　　　律師。1977年旅居台灣，於2003年放棄美
　　　國籍後，歸化為中華民國國籍。

◎撰文（台灣歷史年表）
陳雅文
現職：編輯
學歷：台灣大學歷史系畢業

◎英文審訂
翁佳音
現職：中央研究院台灣史研究所助研究員
學歷：台灣大學歷史研究所碩士，曾留學荷蘭萊頓
　　　大學（Leiden）攻讀歐洲擴張史；專攻十七
　　　、八世紀台灣史

◎英文審訂
賴慈芸
現職：台灣師範大學翻譯研究所助理教授
學歷：香港理工大學中文及雙語研究系博士

◎英文審訂、翻譯
耿柏瑞（Brian A. Kennedy）
現職：博仲法律事務所（本國與外國法事務律師事
　　　務所）編譯員
學歷：美國馬里蘭大學新聞學及東亞學雙學位

◎英文翻譯
范傑克（Jacques Van Wersch）
現職：東森電視新聞事業總部戰略部經理
學歷：加拿大英屬哥倫比亞大學教育學士、加拿大
麥吉爾大學科學學士

◎英文翻譯
白啓賢（Matthew Clarke）
現職：美國密西西比州Nissan公司日語翻譯員
學歷：美國密西根大谷州立大學畢業

◎英文翻譯
賴凱文（Kevin Lax）
現職：專業中英譯者
學歷：英國紐賽大學畢業，主修政治及東亞研究

Editorial Staff

◎Editor-in-Chief,
Author (Ten Short Talks on Taiwan History)

Wu Mi-cha

Wu Mi-cha is an associate professor with National Taiwan University's Department of History.
He received an M.A. degree from the University of Tokyo's Graduate School of Arts and Sciences, specializing in Taiwan history and the history of modern Japan.

◎Chief English Editor

Robin J. Winkler

Robin J. Winkler is director of the Taiwan Wild at Heart Legal Defense Association and founding partner of Winkler Partners, Attorneys of Domestic and Foreign Legal Affairs. Having come to Taiwan in 1977, he gave up his U.S. citizenship to become a naturalized citizen of Taiwan in 2003.

◎Author (Taiwan Timeline)

Grace Chen

Grace Chen works as a newspaper editor. She holds a B.A. degree in history from National Taiwan University.

◎English Editor

Ang Kaim

Ang Kaim is a research fellow at Academia Sinica's Institute of Taiwan History. He received an M.A. degree in history from National Taiwan University. He studied the History of European Expansion at Leiden University in the Netherlands, specializing in the history of Taiwan during the 17th and 18th centuries.

◎English Editor

Sharon Lai

Sharon Lai is assistant professor at the Graduate Institute of Translation and Interpretation, National Taiwan Normal University. She received her Ph.D. in Chinese and bilingual studies from Hong Kong Polytechnic University.

◎English Translator/ Series Editor

Brian A. Kennedy

Brian A. Kennedy is a legal translator for Winkler Partners. He holds a combined B.A. degree in Journalism and East Asian studies from the University of Maryland.

◎English Translator

Jacques Van Wersch

Jacques van Wersch is a Manager in the News Department at Eastern Broadcasting Company.
He received a B.A. in education from the University of British Columbia and a B.S. degree in science from McGill University.

◎英文翻譯
何仁傑（Peter Hillman）
現職：專業中英口譯員
學歷：美國華盛頓州立大學企業管理學士

◎英文翻譯
蘇瑛珣（June Su）
現職：陽明國際律師事務所
學歷：美國加州沛普丹大學法學博士

◎編譯協力
關山行（Mark Brown）
現職：博仲法律事務所（本國與外國法事務律師事務所）法務助理。
學歷：美國德州大學奧斯汀分校（University of Texas at Austin）主修亞洲研究。

◎編譯協力
杜文宇（William A. Dirks）
現職：博仲法律事務所（本國與外國法事務律師事務所）編譯員。
學歷：美國堪薩斯大學東亞研究學系學士，輔仁大學翻譯研究所碩士。

◎編譯協力
馬竣功（Mark D. McVicar）
現職：博仲法律事務所（本國與外國法事務律師事務所）之法務助理及編譯員。
學歷：加拿大滑鐵盧大學歷史系學士、英屬哥倫比亞大學教育學系學士，目前在台灣交通大學攻讀經營管理研究所。

◎編譯協力
羅樂德（Lloyd Roberts III）
現職：博仲法律事務所（本國與外國法事務律師事務所）公共事務部。
學歷：美國奧勒岡大學學士，主修亞洲學，目前在台灣交通大學攻讀經營管理研究所。

◎English Translator
Matthew Clarke
Matthew Clarke is a Japanese translator for Nissan Automotive in Jackson, Mississippi. He holds a B.S. degree in political science from Grand Valley State University in Michigan.

◎English Translator
Kevin Lax
Kevin Lax works as a freelance Chinese-English translator. He graduated with honors with a B.A. in politics and East Asian studies from the University of Newcastle upon Tyne.

◎English Translator
Peter Hillman
Peter Hillman is a freelance Chinese-English interpreter. He received a B.A. degree in business administration from the University of Washington.

◎English Translator
June Su
June Su is an associate attorney with Yang Ming Partners in Taipei. She earned a juris doctorate at Pepperdine University's School of Law.

◎Translation Editor
Mark Brown
Mark Brown is a paralegal with Winkler Partners law firm. He holds a B.A. in Asian Studies from the University of Texas at Austin.

◎Translation Editor
William A. Dirks
William Dirks is a legal translator with Winkler Partners law firm. He holds a B.A. in East Asian Studies from the University of Kansas and an M.A. in Translation and Interpretation Studies from Fu Jen Catholic University in Taipei.

◎Translation Editor
Mark D. McVicar
Mark McVicar is a paralegal and legal translator with Winkler Parnters law firm. He holds a B.A. in History from the University of Waterloo, a B. Ed from the University of British Columbia and is currently pursuing an MBA from the National Chiao Tung University Institute of Business & Management.

◎Translation Editor
Lloyd G. Roberts III
Lloyd Roberts is the Publications and Promotions Associate with Winkler Partners law firm. He holds a B.A. in Asian Studies from the University of Oregon and is currently pursuing an MBA from the National Chiao Tung University Institute of Business & Management.

原《漫畫台灣史》增訂
All new edition

認識台灣歷史
A HISTORY OF TAIWAN IN COMICS

● 總策劃〉吳密察　Editor-in-Chief: Wu Mi-cha

● 英文版策劃〉文魯彬　Chief English Editor: Robin J. Winkler

知識漫畫版・中英對照・全部彩圖演出
Educational comics・Bilingual Chinese-English format・Full-color illustrations

**第一部精采・有趣・
可雙語學習的台灣史**
A fascinating and
compelling bilingual
history of Taiwan

配合教學互動的五大貼心設計

[話說台灣歷史] ●每冊附台大歷史系吳密察教授的精心導讀，輕鬆掌握全書重點與全貌。

[看漫畫學歷史] ●漫畫活潑生動、中英雙語演出，帶領大家從歷史中得到樂趣，從樂趣中了解歷史。

[台灣歷史小百科] ●65則史實與趣聞兼顧的歷史小百科，增加台灣歷史常識。

[台灣歷史年表] ●每冊附台灣歷史大事年表，方便教學和複習。

[台灣歷史常識問答] ●100題激發思考的台灣歷史問答題，方便老師出題、同學相互問答，增加親子話題。

新自然主義股份有限公司
THIRD NATURE PUBLISHING CO., LTD.

Purchasing Information:
http: // www.thirdnature.com.tw

了解台灣，從《認識台灣歷史》開始 A greater understanding of Taiwan starts with "A History of Taiwan in Comics"

1 遠古時代：南島語族的天地
Ancient Times: Austronesian Origins

2 荷蘭時代：冒險者的樂園
The Dutch Era: A Paradise for European Adventurers

3 鄭家時代：鄭氏集團的興衰
The Koxinga Period: The Rise and Fall of the Jheng Regime

4 清朝時代（上）：唐山過台灣
The Cing Dynasty (I): Leaving the Mainland for Taiwan

5 清朝時代（中）：羅漢腳的世界
The Cing Dynasty (II): The World of the "Wandering Bachelors"

6 清朝時代（下）：戰爭陰影下的建設
The Cing Dynasty (III): Construction Under the Shadow of War

7 日本時代（上）：日本資本家的天堂
The Japanese Era (I): The Backyard of Japan's Capitalists

8 日本時代（下）：覺醒的年代
The Japanese Era (II): The Age of Awakening

9 戰後（上）：強人天空下
The Post-World War II Era (I): In the Realm of the Strongmen

10 戰後（下）：改革與開放
The Post-World War II Era (II): Reform and Openness

典藏版10冊＋電子書1片／全套3500元
普及版10冊／全套2500元／全套買省更多，歡迎來電洽詢最新優惠方案。

○○○ 全套買省更多 ○○○

Save even more on a complete set:
Hardcover 10-volume edition + CD-Rom: NT$3500; Paperback 10-volume edition: NT$2500.
Call for details on the latest promotions.

訂購專線：**886-2-27845369**
Call to order: 886-2-27845369

劃撥帳號：**17239354** ／ 新自然主義股份有限公司
Purchasing Information: http:// www.thirdnature.com.tw

感謝專家學者肯定推薦

- 史 英
- 吳密察
- 李 潼
- 李錫津
- 帝瓦伊-撒耘
- 浦忠成
- 馬紹-阿紀
- 高金素梅
- 高榮欽
- 張子樟
- 張炎憲
- 陳建年
- 陳郁秀
- 曾志朗
- 曾憲政
- 動力火車
- 黃光男
- 黃榮村
- 楊孝濚
- 趙自強
- 蔣竹君
- 蔡中涵
- 謝世忠
- 懷劭-法努司

誰最適合閱讀

1. 國小中高年級、國中生最佳課外讀物。
2. 父母家長最新鮮的說故事題材,適合親子共同閱讀。
3. 中小學教師從事原住民教育及原住民母語教學最佳輔助教材。
4. 國內外圖書館、原住民文化展覽館或博物館必備參考書。
5. 發揚及傳承原住民文化的最佳推廣普及工具書。
6. 國外友人,了解台灣原住民文化最佳入門中英對照書。
7. 提供喜愛台灣原住民文化的讀者賞析及珍藏使用。

本書七大特色

1. 傳神生動的台灣原住民故事,搭配色彩豐富的圖畫,讓我們更親近及認識台灣。
2. 結合各族原住民作家採集傳說神話故事,題材多元豐富,並為口傳歷史留下文字見證。
3. 原住民藝術家提供精采插圖,生動呈現傳說故事圖像,令人身歷其境。
4. 每則故事都有中英文對照,並附原住民母語詞彙以及問候語,三種語言一次通。
5. 附「挑戰原住民 Q & A」、「部落百寶盒」、「e 網情報站」方便教師教學與學生複習。
6. 詳解故事精神與意義,萃取原住民生活經驗及與大自然和諧共生的哲理。
7. 古今對照神話故事發生地,附錄各族景點,是學校戶外教學及深度旅遊最佳參考資料。

全系列共10冊

◎ 卑南族:神秘的月形石柱
Mysterious Crescents: Stories from the Puyuma Tribe
故事採集:林志興 / 繪圖‧陳建年

◎ 賽夏族:巴斯達隘傳說
Pas-taai:Legends of the Little People and other Stories from the Saisiat Tribe
故事採集:潘秋榮 / 繪圖‧賴英澤

◎ 布農族:與月亮的約定
Rendezvous with the Moon: Stories from the Bunun Tribe
故事採集:杜石鑾 / 繪圖‧陳景生

◎ 排灣族:巴里的紅眼睛
Pali's Red Eyes and Other Stories from the Paiwan Tribe
故事採集:亞榮隆‧撒可努 / 繪圖‧見維巴里

◎ 邵族:日月潭的長髮精怪
The Long Haired Spirit of Sun Moon Lake: Stories from the Thao Tribe
故事採集:簡史朗 / 繪圖‧陳俊傑

◎ 達悟族:飛魚之神
The Flying Fish Spirit and Other Stories from the Tao Tribe of Orchid Island
故事採集:希南‧巴娜妲燕 / 繪圖‧席‧傑勒吉藍

◎ 泰雅族:彩虹橋的審判
The Rainbow's Judgment: Stories of the Atayal Tribe
故事採集:里慕伊‧阿紀 / 繪圖‧瑁瑁‧瑪邵

◎ 鄒族:復仇的山豬
Revenge of the Mountain Boar and Other Stories from the Cou Tribe
故事採集:巴蘇亞‧迪亞卡納 / 繪圖‧阿伐伊‧尤于伐那

◎ 阿美族:巨人阿里嘎該
Alikakay the Giant and Other Stories from the Amis Tribe
故事採集:馬耀‧基朗 / 繪圖‧林順道

◎ 魯凱族:多情的巴嫩姑娘
Baleng and the Snake: Stories from the Rukai Tribe
故事採集:奧威尼‧卡露斯 / 繪圖‧伊誕‧巴瓦瓦隆

訂購專線:**886-2-27845369**
Call to order: 886-2-27845369

劃撥帳號:**17239354** / 新自然主義股份有限公司
Purchasing Information: http: // www.thirdnature.com.tw

新自然主義公司出版品目錄

＊ 特別推薦系列	作者/譯者/推薦者	定價
NI05 台灣政治學刊(四)－政治變遷與民主化	林佳龍等	250
NI06 新世紀接班人－陳水扁新智囊	陳淞山	260
NI08 台灣政治學刊(五) －政治認知與政策分析	徐永明等	250
NI09 相遇新高雄－海洋首都的蛻變與躍昇	洪美華等	480
NI10 台灣政治學刊(六) －政治變遷與地方自法	黃 紀編	250
NI11 眾神爭奪的國度－走過以色列、巴勒斯坦的戰爭與和平	簡錫堦、徐銘謙	280
NI12 台灣政治學刊－第七卷第一期	吳得源等	250
NI13 台灣醫療發展史	陳永興	450
NI15 台灣政治學刊－第七卷第二期	盛杏湲等	250
NI16 台灣政治學刊－第八卷第一期	王業立等	250
NI17 浪漫高雄－24 小時的深度之旅	鐘順文	280
NI18 台灣政治學刊－第八卷第二期	廖達琪	250
NI19 台灣政治學刊－第九卷第一期	劉義周等	250
＊ 政治研究系列	作者/譯者/推薦者	定價
NL01 派系政治與臺灣政治變遷	陳明通	320
NL08 兩岸社會運動分析	張茂桂等主編	420
＊ 政治社會系列	作者/譯者/推薦者	定價
NM02 新台灣人的心－國家認同的新圖像	蕭新煌	250
NM03 好社會－浩劫後的台灣願景	蕭新煌	250
NM04 新世紀的沈思－政黨輪替前後的觀察與建言	蕭新煌	250
NM05 日出南方－謝長廷執政手記	謝長廷	250
NM06 關鍵年代－陳水扁執政風雲	陳淞山	260
NM07 台灣-分裂國家與民主化	若林正丈	220
NM09 李筱峰專欄-為這個時代留下永遠的歷史見證與記錄	李筱峰	250
NM10 民主 DNA 筆記書-攜手打造－流公民社會	吳英明	230
NM11 新雙城記-謝長廷與馬英九的黃金交叉	林玉珮等編輯群	250
＊ 台灣菁英系列	作者/譯者/推薦者	定價
NP01 油彩精靈陳澄波的故事－台灣美術菁英的生命傳奇	艾米莉編、李俊隆繪	180

* 認識台灣歷史系列 / 總策劃 吳密察 A History of Taiwan' Comics	作者/譯者/推薦者	定價
NR01 認識台灣史(一)－遠古時代	許豐明編寫、劉素珍繪製	250
NR02 認識台灣史(二)－荷蘭時代	許豐明編寫、劉素珍等繪製	250
NR03 認識台灣史(三)－鄭家時代	許豐明編寫、朱鴻琦等繪製	250
NR04 認識台灣史(四)－清朝時代(上)	陳婉菁編寫、朱鴻琦等繪製	250
NR05 認識台灣史(五)－清朝時代(中)	陳婉菁編寫、朱鴻琦等繪製	250
NR06 認識台灣史(六)－清朝時代(下)	謝春馨編寫、朱鴻琦等繪製	250
RF07 認識台灣史(七)－日本時代(上)	鄭承鈞編寫、劉素珍等繪製	250
NR08 認識台灣史(八)－日本時代(下)	鄭丞鈞編寫、劉素珍等繪製	250
NR09 認識台灣史(九)－戰後(上)	何珮琪編寫、劉素珍等繪製	250
NR10 認識台灣史(十)－戰後(下)	何珮琪等編寫、劉素珍等繪製	250
* 台灣原住民的神話與傳說 / 總策劃 孫大川 Traditional Stories from Taiwan's Indigenous Peoples	作者/譯者/推薦者	定價
NC01 卑南族：神秘的月形石柱	林志興採集、陳建年繪製	360
NC02 賽夏族：巴斯達隘傳說	潘秋榮採集、賴英澤繪製	360
NC03 布農族：與月亮的約定	杜石鑾採集、陳景生繪製	360
NC04 排灣族：巴里的紅眼睛	亞榮隆・撒可努採集、見維巴里繪製	360
NC05 邵　族：日月潭的長髮精怪	簡史朗採集、陳俊傑繪製	360
NC06 達悟族：飛魚之神	希南・巴娜姐燕採集、席・傑勒吉藍繪製	360
NC07 泰雅族：彩虹橋的審判	里慕伊・阿紀採集、瑁瑁・瑪邵繪製	360
NC08 鄒　族：復仇的山豬	巴穌亞・迪亞卡那採集、阿伐伊・尤于伐那繪製	360
NC09 阿美族：巨人阿里嘎該	馬耀・基朗採集、林順道繪製	360
NC10 魯凱族：多情的巴嫩姑娘	奧威尼・卡露斯採集、伊誕・巴瓦瓦隆繪製	360
* 播種者系列	作者/譯者/推薦者	定價
HAA01 台灣重層近代化論文集	若林正丈、吳密察　主編	350
HAA02 荷蘭時代台灣的經濟/土地與稅務	韓家寶	220
HAA03 口述歷史	肯・霍爾斯	300
HAA04 十九世紀北部台灣：晚清中國的法律與地方社會	艾馬克	300
HAA05 跨界的台灣史研究：與東亞史的交錯	若林正丈、吳密察　主編	350

訂購專線：886-2-2784-5369　　　　劃撥帳號：17239354 / 新自然主義股份有限公司
Call to Order: 886-2-27845369　　　Purchasing Information: http://www.thirdnature.com.tw

國家圖書館出版品預行編目資料

台灣史10講= Ten Short Talks on Taiwan History
  / 吳密察、陳雅文撰文；耿柏瑞（Brian A.
  Kennedy）等英文翻譯
  .--初版. --臺北市：新自然主義.
  2005〔民94〕 面： 公分
  --（認識台灣歷史精華讀本；上）
  中英對照
  ISBN 957-696-602-7（平裝）

  1. 臺灣 - 歷史 -

673.22   94010337

台灣史10講

Ten Short Talks on Taiwan History

總策劃：吳密察
撰文：吳密察、陳雅文
英文版策劃：文魯彬（Robin J. Winkler）
英文審訂：翁佳音、賴慈芸、耿柏瑞（Brian A. Kennedy）
英文翻譯：耿柏瑞（Brian A. Kennedy）、范傑克（Jacques Van Wersch）、白啟賢（Matthew Clarke）、賴凱文（Kevin Lax）、何仁傑（Peter Hillman）、文魯彬（Robin J. Winkler）、蘇瑛珣（June Su）

初版：2005年7月（2006年7月一版二刷）
定價：新台幣170元
郵撥帳號：17239354 新自然主義股份有限公司
地址：台北市建國南路二段9號10樓之2
電話：886-2-27845369
傳真：886-2-27845358
網址：www.thirdnature.com.tw
E-mail：moonsun@ms18.hinet.net

版權所有・翻印必究 Printed in Taiwan
本書如有缺頁、破損、倒裝，請寄回更換。
ISBN 957-696-602-7

出版者：新自然主義股份有限公司
發行人：洪美華
總編輯：蔡幼華
專案統籌：黃信瑜 / 責任編輯：高美鈴
編譯協力：關山行（Mark Brown）、杜文宇（William A. Dirks）、馬竣功（Mark D. McVicar）、羅樂德（Lloyd Roberts）、王興安、陳明哲、葛窈君、周郁芊、馮瓊儀、黃守義、杜欣欣、吳恬綺
版型設計：唐亞陽工作室 / 美術設計：陳巧玲
編輯部：劉又甄、何靜茹
市場部：張惠卿、劉秀芬、洪秋蓉、黃麗珍
管理部：洪美月、巫毓麗、陳候光、鄭欽祐

製版：凱立國際資訊股份有限公司
印刷：久裕印刷事業股份有限公司

總經銷：農學股份有限公司
台北縣新店市寶橋路235巷6弄6號2樓
電話：886-2-29178022 傳真：886-2-29156275

Call to Order: 886-2-27845369
Website: www.thirdnature.com.tw

特別感謝「博仲法律事務所」（本國與外國法事務律師事務所）的協助。

新自然主義 讀者回函卡

謝謝您購買本書，為加強對讀者的服務並使往後的出書更臻完善，請您詳填本卡各欄，**傳真至（02-27845358）**或投入郵筒寄回（免貼郵票），我們將隨時為您提供最新的出版訊息，以及活動相關資料。

書籍名稱：　《台灣史10講：認識台灣歷史精華讀本（上）》

購買本書的方式：

□01 在＿＿＿＿＿＿ 市（縣）＿＿＿＿＿＿書局購買 □02 劃撥 □03 贈送 □04 展覽、演講活動，名稱＿＿＿＿＿＿ □05 其他＿＿＿＿＿

您從何處得知本書消息？

□01 逛書店 □02 報紙廣告 □03 報紙、雜誌介紹 □04 親友推薦

□05 書訊 □06 廣播節目 □07 新自然主義書友 □08 其他＿＿＿＿＿

您對本書的建議：＿＿＿＿＿＿＿＿＿＿＿＿＿＿＿＿＿＿＿＿＿＿＿

＿＿＿＿＿＿＿＿＿＿＿＿＿＿＿＿＿＿＿＿＿＿＿＿＿＿＿＿＿＿＿

- -

您的個人資料：姓名＿＿＿＿＿＿ 電子信箱：＿＿＿＿＿＿＿＿＿

性別：□男 □女 出生日期：＿＿＿＿＿年＿＿＿＿月＿＿＿日

電話：（＿）＿＿＿＿＿＿＿＿ 傳真：（＿）＿＿＿＿＿＿＿＿

地址：□□□＿＿＿＿＿縣（市）＿＿＿＿鄉鎮區（市）＿＿＿＿路

＿＿＿＿＿街＿＿＿段＿＿＿巷＿＿＿弄＿＿＿號＿＿＿樓

教育程度：□01 小學 □02 國中 □03 高中（職） □04 大專 □05 研究所

□06 其他＿＿＿＿＿

職業：□01 學生 □02 教育 □03 軍警 □04 其他公務 □05 金融業

□06 出版傳播 □07 醫藥 □08 資訊科技 □09 法律工作 □10 其他自由業

□11 其他服務業 □12 製造業 □13 家管 □14 其他＿＿＿＿＿＿

【認識台灣歷史精華讀本】

想要短時間速讀台灣史精華，和朋友天南地北暢談台灣史，

想要和親子一起重溫昔日台灣的古早事，

想要學英文，或是要向外國友人介紹台灣，

【認識台灣歷史精華讀本】肯定是最佳的台灣史讀物。

誠摯邀請大家一起來讀台灣史、了解台灣事。

（請沿線對摺，免貼郵票寄回本公司）

□□□
姓名：
地址：　市　　　鄉鎮
　　　　縣　　市區　　路（街）　　段
　　　　巷　　弄　　　號　　　樓之

廣　告　回　函
北區郵政管理局登記證
北　台　字 5452　號
免　貼　郵　票

新自然主義　股份有限公司

Third Nature Publishing Co., Ltd.

地址：106 台北市建國南路二段 9 號 10 樓之 2
電話：(02)2784-5369　傳真：(02)2784-5358
劃撥：17239354　新自然主義股份有限公司